Understanding

POLICY DOMAINS

their SALIENT

FORCES and

Organisational

Challenges

Tapera O. Chirawu

UNAM PRESS
UNIVERSITY OF NAMIBIA

--

First Published: 2012
University of Namibia Press
Private Bag 13301
Windhoek
Namibia

Language Editors: C. N. S. Shaimemanya & J. Katjavivi
Design and Layout: Printech, Windhoek
Cover Design: John Rittmann
Printed by: Printech, Windhoek

ISBN: 978-99916-870-0-1

Distributed internationally by the African Books Collective: wwwafricanbookscollective.com

For my wife, Maureen, our children

Tapera Jnr, Ngambo, and Tendayi,

and for our last born, Tarisayi Amurefu Chiyuka,

who consistently inspired me to write this book

CONTENTS

ACKNOWLEDGEMENTS

Many people contributed towards the writing of this book. Important to mention are my wife, Maureen, who initiated the idea and advised on the chapter sequencing; Dr C. N. S. Shaimemanya, who used her vast experience as editor of the *Journal of the Namibian Educational Research Association (NERA)* to polish the syntax and the overall language flow; and Ms Jane Katjavivi whose many years' experience in publishing was brought to bear. I sincerely thank them all, including University of Namibia Library staff and others whose roles were also significant. This book could not have been published without their inputs.

LIST OF ABBREVIATIONS

COMESA	Common Monetary Area of Eastern and Southern Africa
ECOWAS	Economic Community of West African States
GNP	Gross National Product
HRMD	Human Resources Management Department
KTDA	Kenya Tea Development Authority
MEC	Ministry of Education and Culture (Namibia)
MRLGH	Ministry of Regional Local Government and Housing (Namibia)
MYNSSC	Ministry of Youth, National Service Sport and Culture (Namibia)
NFSNC	National Food Security and Nutrition Council (Namibia)
NPC	National Planning Commission (Namibia)
OPEC	Organisation of Petroleum Exporting Countries
SACU	Southern Africa Customs Union
SADC	Southern Africa Development Commission
UNO	United Nations Organisation

PREFACE

Policies are about human behaviour. They focus on access to and delivery of goods and services, and aim to ensure human security. Their major natural domains are fauna and flora, topography, and factors of demography, within which one encounters individual, group, and institutional programmes and objectives, dictated by human life necessities. These determine the context of policy:

- the past that shaped present human behaviour;
- the quantities and quality of goods and services needed then, now and tomorrow; and
- the present that, in turn, determines citizens' future behaviour, aimed at constantly obtaining life requirements in sufficient quantities.

The past, the present and the future constitute salient forces of policy that largely determine political, social and economic policy activities. These three elements of time exist in a symbiotic relationship, depicting a necessary incremental accumulation of knowledge and experience that explains human development under different environments.

Societies need systems and instruments to produce and supervise distribution of goods and services to the people. Policies are such instruments. They ensure citizens' compliance with governments' intentions as per their constitutional mandate to achieve service equity. Given the multiplicity of policy causes that largely comprise deprivations, threats and efforts to fulfil political challenges and promises, policy processes respond to social sector demands that differ in scope and solution requirements. Hence, it is necessary to distinguish between internal and external causes, and between national and local causes as the response to each differs situationally and contextually.

Policies also manifest in different constituencies, each of which has its own characteristics and challenges. Governments and organisations need to understand these in order to strategically situate their operations and make them viable. The challenges provoke a continuous search for solutions, the objective of which is to secure effective behavioural change, informed by past and present life experiences and demands. Success requires community or national consensus and commitment to the suggested policy programme. Personal perceptions of policy, political action, leadership integrity, and situational use of force, drive the process, which faces challenges of consensus, legitimacy, scarcity of resources, and sustainability. Nevertheless, families, communities, organisations and governments need policies of different typologies in order to meet their institutional mandates.

Public policy making is a daunting task involving competing interests; a legion of opportunities to proffer solutions to social, political, and economic problems; a locus of contradicting interpretations of social concerns and possible remedies; and a potential instrument to enhance human endeavours and prepare for a sustainable higher quality of life. It should, in addition, provide lenses through which the ordinary citizenry can realise quantitative improvement in the requirements for satisfactory individual and collective life expectancy.

Policy making as a process should seek to maximally benefit from the intellectual wisdom that directs institutional action, to achieve good governance, as it is undertaken in an ever-changing political environment. The process should recognise that within every society political parties serve as 'basic institutions for the translation of mass preferences into public policy' (Lindblom & Woodhouse, 1993, p. 136). At the same time, the process should not overlook the negative side: that politics obstruct learning, misrepresent issues, and insulate elected officials from genuine accountability, thereby facilitating governments to subjugate, tyrannise, promote some groups' welfare over that of others, and favour well-organised interest groups over the shared needs of the citizenry as a whole (p. 137). All is done through the policy process.

In addition to directing organisational operations as an institutional function, policy making is also a function of democracy, which requires that community members should provide information on issues that concern their lives. In the process, policy making should involve elected community representatives. The elections require policies that guarantee politics of inclusivity, transparency, and accountability. In other words, policies focus on the behaviour of people and institutions. The objective cannot be easily achieved, however, because policy formulation is a challenge to democracy and to political fair play. It acknowledges the need to have broad views on every issue but may not necessarily incorporate all of them in the final outcome. It also recognises that contestations surround every policy process. These include:

- the purposive insulation of office holders;
- bias in favour of interest and business groups;
- easier access to higher echelons of power for leaders of organisation than for ordinary citizens;
- the differentiation of information dissemination by social strata; and
- the unequal distribution of economic resources (Lindblom & Woodhouse, 1993).

That leaves the ordinary citizen unable to revamp an iniquitous political situation in which inequalities, government's non-response, social and political frustration among the people, and general deterioration of security and life quality become the order of the day.

Policy process is at the root of the day-to-day activities of every institution and government, particularly in Africa. As an element of planning, it helps to segregate competing interests and demands, as well as social and economic compulsions. It also makes it possible to prioritise programme selection in a way that ensures efficient implementation and achievement of the desired results. However, the attainment or non-attainment of policy objectives is a result of the relationships involving competing social, political and economic ideologies locally and internationally. In Africa, such competition involves political parties, some of which are alleged to be externally sponsored. That helps to explain the interlocking factors of policy causation. African political parties owe their existence to their history, in particular that which concerns the liberation struggle, and to the acceptance and effectiveness of the programmes they put in place when their countries attained independence. However, these programmes are usually tied to the next general elections. Viewed through the ideological 'isms' and leadership patterns with which Ghana, Kenya, Malawi, Mali, Mozambique, Namibia, Nigeria, Tanzania, Zambia, and Zimbabwe are identified, a plethora of policies made it possible for developmental infrastructure to be built. Governments, non-governmental organisations (NGOs), and the private sector were all involved (Blunt, Jones, & Richards, 1993; Angula & Bankie, 2000; Gibbon *et al.* 1992; Mukwena & Chirawu, 2008). Their combined effort produced hospitals, schools, communication and recreational facilities, and food outlets in both urban and rural areas.

Individual leaders' interests also constitute a major policy making factor, as has been seen in these countries. When bombarded from within with allegations of incompetence, and from outside by allegations of human rights abuse, and when threatened by citizens' (demands for democratic change, African leaders use government machinery to protect themselves. The instruments employed are the legislature and security units (police, military, and intelligence or special unit forces). Another is the Ministry of Home Affairs, which controls people's movement, including entry into and exit from the country concerned. These are purposive instruments to provide and protect public order, but also to provide and protect policies that are designed to advance personal agendas, in particular when a leadership's popularity is waning. In Africa examples are many (Gibbon *et al.* 1992).

Private businesses also manifest policy demands, because they translate themselves into votes by using their inexhaustible resources. The same applies to individual citizens, because they represent personal interests that strive to be heard on a continuous basis (Lindblom & Woodhouse, 1993). Their votes can remove a government from power. Therefore, neither individual political leaders nor governments as institutions can afford to ignore them and hope to receive their votes during subsequent general elections.

Furthermore, group attachment, which obliges individuals to respond to and address family members' social and economic concerns, is yet another major policy factor. It is a known fact that the 'economics of affection' in African tradition compel stakeholders not to deviate, else they isolate themselves from the only social and political constituency that guarantees economic and social support. As Vansina (1965) discovered during his research on Africa's oral traditions, policies based on traditional and customary ties are largely not written, yet they are followed to the letter.

Finally, the political condensing of the world into a global village has eliminated whatever space there was for national policies to be independently viable. Overall national security now largely rests on conforming with international social, political, economic, and security compulsions; leaving the renegades to suffer. Zimbabwe's economic meltdown between 2000 and 2009 is a good attestation to this (Walker and Agencies, 2008).

These life challenges necessitate crafting institutional and/or government policies holistically, informed by community, regional, national and international life factors that depict verifiable challenges to human development and life sustenance.

This book is an effort to identify, and simplify, the policy factors that underline the success or failure of governments and institutions.

References

Angula, N. & Bankie, B. F. (2000) (Eds). *The African Origin of Civilisation and the Destiny of Africa.* Windhoek:

Blunt, P., Jones, M. L. & Richards, D. (1993). *Managing Organisations in Africa: Readings, Cases, and Exercises.* New York: Walter de Gruyter.

Gibbon, P., Bangura, Y. & Ofstad, A. (1992) (Eds). *Authoritarianism, Democracy, and Adjustment – The Politics of Economic Reform in Africa.* Uppsala: The Scandinavian Institute of African Studies.

Lindblom, C. E. & Woodhouse, E. J. (1993). *Public Policy Making.* (Third Edition) Englewood Cliffs, NJ: Prentice Hall.

Mukwena, R. & Chirawu, T. (2008) (Eds). *Decentralisation and Regional and Local Government in Namibia.* Windhoek: R. Mukwena and T. Chirawu.

Vansina, J. (1965). *Oral Traditions: A Study in Historical Methodology.* Chicago: Aldine Publishing.

Walker, Peter and Agencies (2008). Zimbabwe inflation soars to 2.2m%. Retrieved 30 May 2009 from http://www.guardian.co.uk/world/2008/jul/16/zimbabwe.

1

INTRODUCTION

Without policies, chaos would reign, to the disadvantage of organisational plans and human life conditions, in a manifestation of unending struggle for survival and quest for solutions too challenging to accomplish.

Policies drive institutional operations worldwide. They are behavioural instruments for the living – animals and human beings alike. They represent life's instinctive compulsion for the peaceful distribution, receipt, and use of goods and services among community members, and the maintenance of peace and security.

Although the method of delivery and receipt of goods and services is expected to come with equal opportunities and access to life-supporting variables, natural and man-made structures and levels of authority manifest. Furthermore, situations that prompt policies are observed at different levels of society before a government takes on the responsibility of addressing whatever challenges these situations pose. The communities that make up society constitute the constituencies of traditions and customs, which provide the basis for the rules and regulations that guide the behaviour of each and every community member. In short, traditions and customs define and explain every member's place in the community. The member's identification and behavioural characteristics are embedded not only in the collectivity of the same kind, but also in all the things that contribute towards the shaping, controlling, and protecting of the group members. Hence, the history and nature of the group relationships, as well as their value and current contribution to life, is proof enough that 'familiarity breeds respect and practice creates its own legitimacy' (Parenti, 1978, p.124).

Policies prescribe how one should act when faced with a situation. Lessons can be drawn from the human and animal kingdoms, traditions, customs, and practices in Africa over the past many centuries. In the animal kingdom, the cubs of a dethroned king of a pride of lions are killed in order to ensure that the new cubs or offspring are those of the new leader (Mad Mike & Mark, Animal Planet TV Channel, 2008). It is indeed a testimony that 'Institutionally controlled roles are legitimised by practice and familiarity which disguise their coercive elements' (Parenti, 1978, p. 133). What contributes to the identity of the collectivity includes a sense of 'rationally [joining] together to form civil society. Society thus, arising naturally out of fear,' and indeed in the quest for personal security (Hobbes quoted in Roskin *et al.* 2000, p. 23).

Additionally, inasmuch as one cannot practically separate any of the elements of the physical environment, namely fauna and flora, man and different types of living things, from the others, one cannot separate the dead from the living. The two are bonded to each other by history, tradition and blood, beckoning the southern Sudanese leader, John Garang, to make his statement at the 7th Pan African Congress in Kampala in 1994, when he referred to the liberation struggle in Africa as being characterised by the fact that 'The dead are not dead, and the living are not living.' The statement comprehensively summarises the feelings and emotions that the formerly colonised citizens have about colonialism and its legacy. It also underlines the fact that the present is what it is because of past policies, and that today's policies shape the future in a web of intricate social, political, and economic relations. There could not be a better attestation of the link between those who have come and gone, those who are alive today, and those still to be born. Hence, Africans' unflinching attachment to their ancestral graveyards and other historic sites helps to explain genealogical lineages. As a result, intense opposition to the levelling of graveyards never ends (Namibia: Epupa Dam Study, 1998; National Society for Human Rights, no date).

The struggle for land in former colonies put aside, Professor Wangari Maathai took on former Kenyan President Arap Moi's security forces as she protested (on environmental grounds) against turning Nairobi's 'Uhuru Park' into a business development site (Maathai, Wangari, 2009). Ugandans took a similar route in April 2007 as they opposed an Indian owned Sugar Corporation of Uganda that planned to take over 7,000 hectares (17,000 acres) of Mabira Forest Reserve (Riots in Uganda, 2007). In both cases government, in spite of being an embodiment of society, triggered hostile responses from some groups whose interests were entrenched in history and practice. These phenomena demonstrate the vulnerability of policy to many factors, which include:

- living people as individuals, or in different situational and/or social formations;
- dead people's legacies or relationships with the living, anywhere and everywhere on earth;
- fauna and flora world-wide; and
- natural phenomena such as deserts, floods, drought, lightening and volcanic eruptions.

The impact of each of these factors is topographically selective as determined by the susceptibility and/or vulnerability of the areas or people affected. The scenarios thus inform us that complex environments provide habitats to policy processes, and that there are many constituents of policy causes.

⅃ Flora

⑃ flora represent the animal and vegetation life that is a necessity of human
as a source of economic survival, food and energy. They also contribute towards
.l balance, in that they constitute a life-giving environment which, more than any
, guarantees the continuity of human, animal, and plant life. They must be protected
ınrough policies, or their destruction and possible extinction because of deforestation and
killing (for meat and other purposes) could affect human life security. People know this,
so they seek to protect fauna and flora by establishing game parks, zoos, aquariums, and
aviaries, not to mention societies for preventing cruelty to animals. As the UN General
Assembly (1992) has resolved:

> Forest resources and forest lands should be sustainably
> managed to meet the social, economic, ecological and
> spiritual needs or services, such as wood products,
> water, food, fodder, medicine, fuel, shelter, employment,
> recreation, habitats for wildlife birds and animals,
> landscape diversity, carbon sinks and reservoirs, and
> other forest products.

The value and sustenance of each of the factors of life mentioned above require visionary
strategies built into instruments that control human behaviour. The instruments largely
compromise policies, rules and regulations. These must be reviewed regularly in order
to ensure they are serving the purpose for which they were designed, and that they are
keeping up with or timeously responding to whatever situational changes take place.

Animals, reptiles, birds, a large variety of bees and many species of flying insects, as well
as other different types of living things, are major agents of natural ecological balance, in
which each species' instinctive survival habits play an important role Their behaviour, if
not controlled by nature or by human beings, could cause the extinction of some species,
and the overpopulation of others; and overpopulation naturally leads to self-destruction
due to food shortages or endemic diseases. Both the extinction of some species and the
overpopulation of others are threats to the balance of nature and, indeed, to human
survival. Hence, the need for policy controls. However much we may want to control
deadly cyclones, hurricanes, tornadoes, whirlwinds, earthquakes, volcanic eruptions,
lightning, floods, droughts, and terminal diseases (such as cancer and HIV/AIDS), we are
not yet scientifically advanced enough to offer meaningful preventive measures besides
policies that control human behaviour and focus on our protection through avoidance,
minimizing negative impacts, and limiting damage.

The ecological natural balancing act provokes a host of issues that pose serious challenges
to the capacity of human beings for self-protection. However, the concept of self-protection

can be clearly understood only through the relationships discussed earlier: that fau
the flora for food, medicine and protection; and that each species needs the othei
food and the security that comes with group membership. As a result, individual intere
dominate group discussions on policies of procedural, regulatory, or self-regulatoi
typologies.

Important to note, is that self-protection manifests through relationships of dependency. It is the natural lack of self sufficiency of every living thing that underpins the necessity to network in order to survive, that best describes 'dependency theory' (Bayat, 1993; Weatherby et al. 2000; Giddens, 1993). The theory explains that individuals, groups, communities and nations have needs caused by nature and by people, and that these needs must be provided for in ways that explain the non-self-sufficient nature of human survival. That is, every living thing depends on the willingness of other living things to provide, in a symbiotic relationship in which no living thing can provide everything for itself. It is, therefore, necessary to fully understand what policy seeks to probe – the human psychological mix comprising greed, empathy, threat, and natural compulsion for co-existence, through behavioural patterns and adaptation to natural environmental conditions. It is also important to bear in mind that the symbiosis is not necessarily harmonious. Some living things need other living things as food; and a crimeless society would signal the arrival of utopia. Policy process is, therefore, a timeless phenomenon that requires timely responses to situational challenges, and to the dictates of environmental changes.

Discussion of the necessity for goods and services departs from the premise that public policies are created to meet perceived national needs (Roskin et al. 2000, pp. 322-3), by way of influencing individual and group behaviour to initiate the production and delivery of needed goods and services in desired quantities, and to do so reliably and consistently. It is also logical that legislative decisions, judiciary rulings, executive decrees and, most importantly, administrative decisions, are inextricable components of the policy process, in particular in terms of policy implementation, adjudication and evaluation (Roskin et al. 2000). Furthermore, it is important to note that sociological and economic inequalities are at the centre of policy process, mostly because of the necessity to provide the needs during policy implementation, and the compulsion to control human actions that guide the provision of the needs. Each 'need' has its own influence on human behaviour.

Policy deals with perceptions about life, and the relationship between its major components. These are normally physical or psychological. Policies also react to life requirements, prompting Greenberg and Baron (2000) to identify social influence as a key element of policy implementation. It is, thus, the nature of the influences that shapes the perceptions, and the need to translate those perceptions into human behaviour that necessitates policy. This, in turn, points to the necessity to understand the purpose of policy: in what exact way or manner is policy designed to impact on the numerous situational phenomena that influence socio-economic and political formations in society, thereby compelling different institutions and governments to control citizens' behaviour?

Some of the available literature clearly indicates that policy purpose is to empower and integrate government institutions so that they can mobilise the resources they need to use and equitably provide services in a co-coordinated manner. Consequently, organisational accountability and the effort to institutionalise democracy become prerequisites, because a government without policies that guarantee institutional accountability can neither empower its citizens nor ensure good governance (Ministry of Youth, National Service, Sport and Culture, no date; Malawi Decentralisation Secretariat, no date; National Planning Commission, 1997; Southern African Regional Institute for Policy Studies, 1995; Ministry of Education and Culture, 1993; National Food Security and Nutrition Council 1995; Ministry of Regional Local Government Housing, 1998; Robbins and Decenzo, 2004).

The convergence of the opinions and perceptions underline the universality of the characteristics, and the commonality of the social, political, and economic nature of services that society needs. Therefore, each policy element must be studied and understood on its own in order to correctly know the extent to which it impacts on the overall policy process, vis-à-vis reliability and consistency of the delivery of goods and services needed.

With regards to society, Roskin *et al.* (2000, p. 30) argue that 'if there were a book entitled "The Political Basis of Society," such a book would posit society as largely the result of political institutions formed and decisions made over the decades.' This statement implies not only that social formations or people living within the same biotope (Vansina, 1965) result from demographic and economic factors, but also that personal and group interests are central to decision making, and that decision making is embedded in political processes. Therefore, social formations signify common desires and the need to satisfy those desires. The latter is generally the responsibility of political process which, by necessity, involves policies. This means that every society comprises social formations that survive through policies that control and guide the behaviour of each and every member.

Behaviour is a human function that indicates or implies negative or positive reaction to a given situation. It is always associated with initiating, wanting, searching, getting, receipt, using, or rejecting. 'People have basic needs and thus they desire those material goods that satisfy the needs. Moreover, people by themselves cannot provide for these needs. So societies are formed for this purpose' (DeLue, 1997, pp. 33-4). Glaucon, quoted in DeLue (1997, p. 43), went further to suggest that, 'People will want luxuries as well as having their basic needs satisfied;' and, 'for needs, material and luxuries to have meaningful value, there must be artefacts, jewellery for women, music and dance, as well as leisure time.' Consequently, the purpose of policy is to create an environment in which members of the society are empowered to determine and provide through their organisations or government, the needs and material the society wants. At the same time, policies must be formulated to regulate and control the processes designed to deliver the services in a way that ensures efficiency, equity, consistency and reliability. Therefore, policy process must not only create a desired environment, but must also bind behaviour to acceptable uniform conduct that allows for equal access to amenities and the just receipt of benefits the society and natural resources offer. Effective synergies of the same should provide a necessary catalyst for a successful policy process.

In addition, some researched and expertly analysed work on management proffers evidence that administration is a systematic process of making decisions, based on clear organisational policies that provide for impromptu action, dictated by perceived, situational, expected and unexpected phenomena that call for government action to provide solutions (Henry, 2001; Fox *et al.* 1991; Blunt & Jones, 1992; Parker, 2003). The definition partially borrows from McGregor's Theory X assumption about human behaviour towards work (Schein, 1994). Theory X says that unless people are closely supervised, they will not execute their tasks. Most importantly, the definition takes cognisance of the 'values the members of a given group hold, the norms they follow, and the material goods they create...indeed the most distinctive properties of human social association' (Giddens, 1993, pp. 31-2, 740). These generally characterise cultural perceptions about life, and influence particular positions that communities take in any policy process. To be noted is the fact that desires, expected and unexpected phenomena, and perceptions, exist in the abstract sphere until they have been converted/translated into concrete and realisable outputs of thoughts analysing the causes of a given situation – until they evolve into policy issues. Until then, they are intangible manifestations of imagined possible happenings that policy process may seek to define by analysing the behaviour of those who are affected. Hence, policy process within a cultural setting could be considered as an effort to achieve exclusive desirable life conditions. It could also be an endeavour to correct what might be wrong in society, or to improve the quality of life generally. In other words, people can initiate activities which they think will qualitatively and quantitatively enhance the standard of living in their communities. However, the initiatives can succeed only if the community gives its support; that is if the community agrees with the policy objectives.

Furthermore, human behaviour is also a barometer of the acceptability or non-acceptability of what is either perceived or actually practiced in society. It is an indicator of people's response to what is given or is being practiced, although it does not have the support of every community member, regardless of how attractive it may be. Hence, social, political, economic and cultural compulsions constitute the bond among interlocking elements of the policy process, namely: administration, which is an embedment of the 'abstract-sphere'; the 'practical sphere' which is an exposition of action; and the policy outcome – what Anderson (2003, p. 249) calls 'The consequences for society, intended and unintended, that stem from deliberate [governmental] action or inaction'.

The 'practical sphere' of policy process is the conversion of the life perceptions (ideas and interpretation of those ideas) into work plans with clear vertical (hierarchical organisational order) and horizontal synergies (lateral and symbiotic information sharing designed to prevent duplication). The conversion is, in actuality, the act of management, which entails converting policies into action with clear objectives. That means *working with and through individuals and groups to accomplish organisational goals* (Robbins and Decenzo, 2004). It all begins with people's perceptions developed into coherent issues constituting policy foundation. Natural phenomena also provide policy foundations, as mentioned earlier. Therefore, policy process requires an implementation plan indicating logical and sequential activities that provide clear intention and purpose of action. That entails:

1   communicating the concerns;
2   estimating policy objectives;
3   determining the work plan;
4   determining the scope of the implementation programme;
5   identifying the necessary inputs;
6   providing the schedule; and
7   giving instructions, orders and/or commands for practical work to be done; at the same time cheques must be signed to pay for the cost of the work completed or still in progress.

These activities should collaboratively lead to the attainment of policy objectives and desirable policy output, in particular the realisation of the cardinal attributes of life quality. These include good governance, recognition of individual rights to participate in the national policy process, respect for human rights and dignity, equitable provision of goods and services, and making available any other situational and institutional requirements necessary for human life.

It should further be noted that an individual's needs manifest through social, political and economic relations prevailing within the family, community, tribe, and society that one is part of. A member of a well-to-do family can be forgiven for wanting today's luxuries – a car, television, cell phone, etc. At the same time, a member of an economically average community would be contented with less expensive accommodation, clothing, and means of transport because he/she knows that it is all he/she can afford. Similarly, belonging to a tribe that is historically and traditionally on the economic fringes of the mainstream society brings limited ambitions and constrained initiatives. Such belonging could be a manifestation of a lifetime vicious circle that represents comprehensive deprivation that is difficult to break out of. Hence, the position that one occupies in society largely determines where one stands on a particular policy issue (Beckman, 1984). Therefore, an individual's needs, namely 'norms and networks that enable people to act collectively' are an exposition of life perceptions reflecting different levels of social capital (Portes, 1998, pp. 1-24). One's economic status and social as well as traditional belonging work in tandem and determine norms and net workings. Policy process interprets and translates these into administrative expressions that are concretised through managerial work plans and programmes, of which the output provides quantifiable results. The connectivity of the administrative expressions (abstract sphere), the work plans and programmes (management), and the results (objectives), summarises the policy process (see figure 1 on page 9).

It is important to note that the nature of the cause, time and space determine policy characteristics. The features of the characteristics arise from the general policy orientation, such as focus specificities.

Policy Causes

Policy causes are largely embedded in the society's needs delivery matrix, supported by the elements and traditional human behaviour control systems. Constituting the matrix are social, political, and economic factors; the dictates of nature – droughts, floods, diseases, volcanic eruptions; and a combination of pests and animals, both domesticated and wild. The causes manifest in various combinations that require measured response within specific parameters and demographic settings. The scope largely provides the variables at play. The following possible scenarios serve as some examples.

Scenario 1

Suppose a demonstration is held to protest about a lack of accommodation on a university campus. The majority of the protesters are foreign students, and it might be expected that only those failing to secure accommodation would get involved. However, they could be joined by local students claiming that the food the university serves is also poor, given the high fees that they pay, thus confusing the cause and complicating the possible solution. Should the quality of food become the dominant cause of the demonstration, it might be that the more vocal and articulate students who push this problem to the forefront come from well-to-do homes. They may be used to better food than that provided by the university, thereby presenting an external social class factor, and characterising the complexity and nature of the overall cause. That could determine the kind of policy to emerge after the demonstration, which might reflect and represent minority interests. However, the institution concerned could also choose to formulate a comprehensive policy covering all the major issues deciphered from the causes of the demonstrations, namely shortage of accommodation, quality of food, and others. Such a policy would have broad parameters in terms of the target group and services to be provided.

Scenario 2

When nature intervenes in the intricate relations between the demands of human life and the elements of the natural environment, this usually prompts immediate evaluation of human behaviour, either as a contributing factor to the situation, or in terms of possible victims. For example, if a bridge built on the outskirts of a city collapses and water floods

Figure 1: Policy Process Synergies

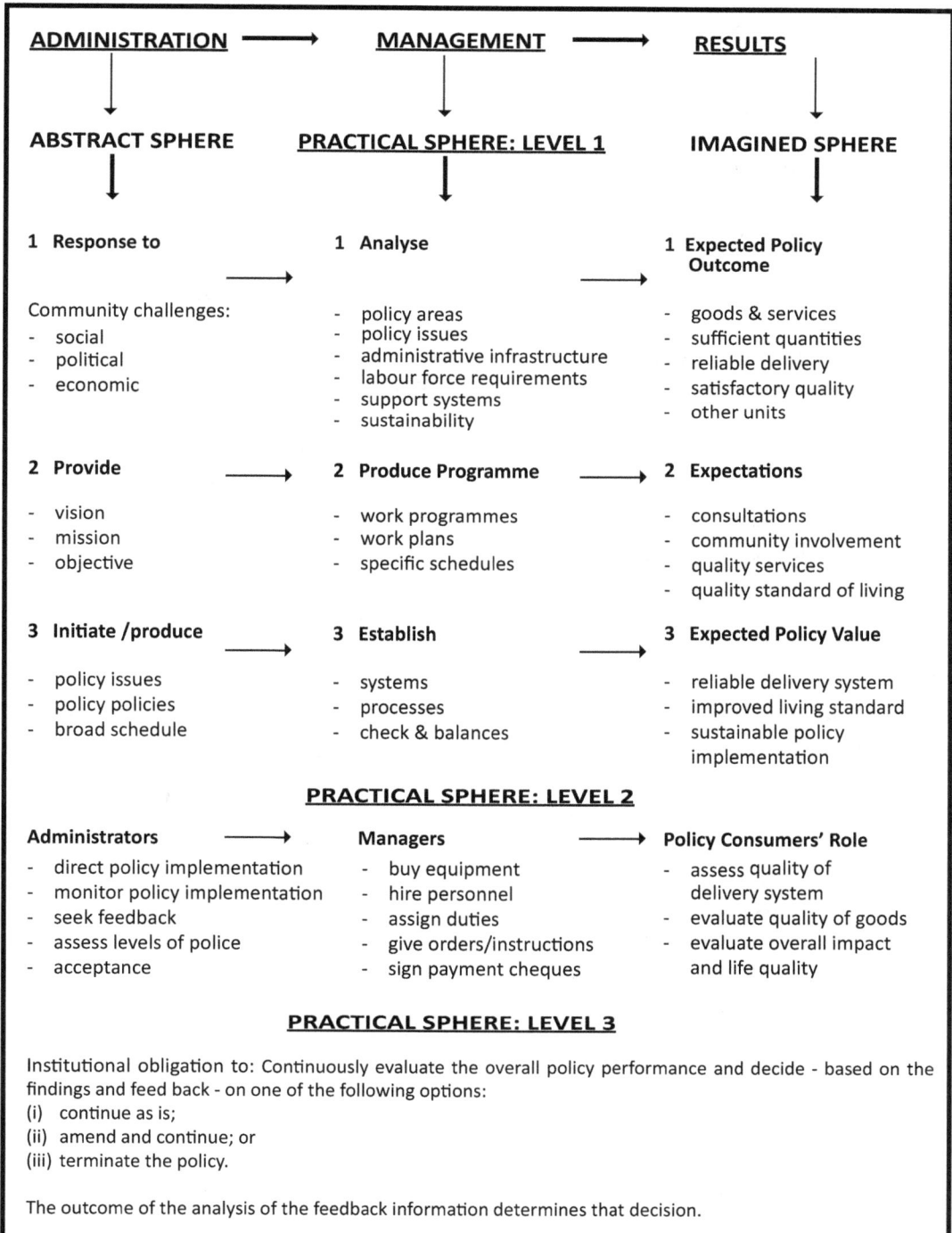

ADMINISTRATION →	MANAGEMENT →	RESULTS
↓	↓	↓
ABSTRACT SPHERE	**PRACTICAL SPHERE: LEVEL 1**	**IMAGINED SPHERE**
↓	↓	↓

1 Response to →	**1 Analyse** →	**1 Expected Policy Outcome**
Community challenges: - social - political - economic	- policy areas - policy issues - administrative infrastructure - labour force requirements - support systems - sustainability	- goods & services - sufficient quantities - reliable delivery - satisfactory quality - other units
2 Provide →	**2 Produce Programme** →	**2 Expectations**
- vision - mission - objective	- work programmes - work plans - specific schedules	- consultations - community involvement - quality services - quality standard of living
3 Initiate /produce →	**3 Establish** →	**3 Expected Policy Value**
- policy issues - policy policies - broad schedule	- systems - processes - check & balances	- reliable delivery system - improved living standard - sustainable policy implementation

PRACTICAL SPHERE: LEVEL 2

Administrators →	Managers →	Policy Consumers' Role
- direct policy implementation - monitor policy implementation - seek feedback - assess levels of police - acceptance	- buy equipment - hire personnel - assign duties - give orders/instructions - sign payment cheques	- assess quality of delivery system - evaluate quality of goods - evaluate overall impact and life quality

PRACTICAL SPHERE: LEVEL 3

Institutional obligation to: Continuously evaluate the overall policy performance and decide - based on the findings and feed back - on one of the following options:
(i) continue as is;
(ii) amend and continue; or
(iii) terminate the policy.

The outcome of the analysis of the feedback information determines that decision.

the city, causing great damage, any of the following factors could be the cause, as could a combination of them.

- the technology used in constructing the bridge;
- the age of the bridge;
- management of the bridge – how frequently it is serviced;
- monitoring of the water levels;
- work conditions (salary and other benefits) for the personnel responsible for monitoring the water levels;
- supervision of the personnel;
- monitoring of the weather patterns; and
- the proximity of the bridge to the city could also be a factor.

An investigation of the situation could reveal that human error during the construction of the bridge, or human behaviour resulting from either work conditions or pure negligence, was to blame. At the same time, the simple superior strength of nature over human intelligence and efforts could have caused the catastrophe. Whatever might be the case, a possible solution would lie in the ability of the relevant institutions to isolate the cause and institute policies to control human behaviour either preventively or correctively. Such policies would need to target the consumers in relation to demographic factors, time, operational scope and parameters, service provision schedules, consistence of the delivery, reliability of the service providers, and the quality of the goods and services.

As policy is made for all time, the majority of the 'gurus' on policy (Anderson, 2003; Fox *et al.* 1991; Lindblom and Woodhouse, 1993) agree on the following stages, which involve a wide range of stakeholders. These stages are:

- environmental scanning
- policy advocacy
- agenda setting
- consideration of options
- making the policy choice
- publicising
- adopting
- crafting the implementation programme
- costing
- resource allocation
- implementing/managing/monitoring
- adjudication, and
- evaluation.

Corrective measures entail a policy process indicated in figure 2 on page 11.

Figure 2: Policy Process from Initiation to Evaluation

1	SITUATION	Is something observable happening? Yes, but not necessarily physical activities.
2	STRONG IMPRESSION	Strong conviction that the situation is either not acceptable, or that it can be changed for the better.
3	CONVERT THE IMPRESSIONS INTO ISSUES	Translate the information creating the impressions into specific issues, or items for debate.
4	CATEGORISE THE ISSUES	Discuss and prioritise the issues in order of how each affects or influences life or organisational designs and activities
5	PROCESS THE ISSUES	Compare and contrast the issues, and prioritise them in terms of how each impacts on the current and future desired benefits.
6	MAKE THE CHOICE	Determine and select the most beneficial alternative.
7	PUBLICISE	Present the choice to society and involve the citizens in the selection. People's preferences should provide the answer.
8	ADOPTION	Policy makers are agents of society. What society decides, is what must be done.
9	DESIGN ACTION PLAN	Policy implementation requires a clear programme that can be monitored and evaluated. Activities and their synergies must be clearly articulated, including costing
10	IMPLEMENTATION	Orders and instructions must be given for the work to be done. Cheques must be signed to pay for accomplished tasks. Personnel must be trained and new technology and other necessary equipment acquired.
11	ADJUDICATION	Management must ensure that the implementation tasks are carried out as planned, and that those who deviate are punished.
12	MONITORING AND CONTROL	Built-in instruments to ensure that schedules are met and specific behaviour that guarantees work consistency and continuity collaborates with the implementation and adjudication work output.
13	IMPACT EVALUATION	Assessment of the correctness, sufficiency, and effectiveness of all the inputs, namely information and material at every level and stage of the process, is continuously done right from the beginning. It is to determine the peoples' immediate response to the policy.
14	POLICY EVALUATION	A comprehensive assessment not of the immediate response to the policy, but of the whole policy process: • Quality of the initial information explaining and motivating the demand for policy. • Quality of the debate when determining and categorising the issues. • Quality of the schedules-activities and costs. • Quality of services and benefits therefrom, and • Prospective sustainability of the policy.

Source: Adapted from Lindblom & Woodhouse, 1993; Anderson, 2003; Fox, *et al.,* 1991.

Ordinary citizens representing all walks of life, namely professionals (academicians and lawyers), religious leaders, technocrats and bureaucrats, politicians, students, news media personnel, and representatives of different public, private, as well as non-governmental organisations, contribute in multi-faceted ways. They do so because each and every citizen and, indeed, each and every organisation, individually and collectively, experience the positive and negative effects of life phenomena. Firstly, their involvement in the policy process is engendered by each and every citizen's need for services. Secondly, the value of an individual's behaviour manifests through linkages with other human beings' behaviour. Hence, the meaning and identity of a policy can be understood only through the lifespan of those who formulate and implement it, and those who are recipients of the services it provides. This can be measured not in a day but over a considerable period of time. It is only then that a complete policy performance can be evaluated, and its necessity and value to society determined.

Time and Space

The relationship between space and policy is the same as that between water and a wide, long, and meandering deep gully on earth, that widens when the sand on its edges (banks) falls in and gets washed away, or fills up when water sweeps sand and rubbish from catchment areas into the gully, leaving no room for the water to collect and stay. We call such a gully a river. For a river to widen, the topography must be of the type that allows the water to run only in specific directions. Similarly, policies are demand-oriented actions designed to facilitate provision and receipt of goods and services, or to protect consumers from undesirable situations caused by people through theft, corruption, deforestation, gender bias or violence, or by nature. Therefore, the causes of policy are characterised by distinct human needs and/or desires, manifesting within clearly identifiable relationships and linkages between the two major stakeholders – human beings and nature.

Human desires do not occur in a vacuum. They are definable only within a given space and identifiable time span. Occupation of space is characterised by a policy's existence among competing species of a similar type, namely institutional rules and regulations that are also instruments designed to control human behaviour. By the same token, consumers must have the opportunity to abide by or defy a new policy, while they are concurrently dealing with the many other rules and regulations that govern their behaviour. That means the policy must command legitimacy and legal institutional adjudication within national or territorial boundaries. Hence, a policy cannot be enforced outside the space within which it is an acceptable behavioural control instrument. In the same vein, time is characterised by how long it takes for the stakeholders to know about the policy (through political and educational efforts by other people), and to understand its general implications and effect on society. In addition, different institutions must be afforded the opportunity to evaluate the fairness, implementability, as well as the worth of the policy.

On the whole, research and practical experience inform us that knowledge about human life, nature, time and space are the pillars of policy process and policy habitat. They are distinguished by an abstract sphere (human intellect), purposive management plans, and an imagined outcome, as their operational elements. These, in turn, provide the arena in which the compulsions for cultural, traditional, social, political and economic belonging bind every individual as an individual, or as a member of a non-governmental organisation or government Ministry, to the provisions of every public policy. They also provide for the understanding of the synergy between citizens and institutional control measures designed to ensure peaceful co-existence and community development in the country, by way of identifying policy issues and translating them into acceptable, implementable, and sustainable programmes.

Conclusion

This chapter has argued that individual, group and institutional needs manifest within recognisable factors of nature, in an interaction between the effects of weather and topography on one hand, and demography, culture and tradition on the other. In so doing, the natural superiority of humankind over most of God's creations enables us to establish, through institutional policies, an equilibrium that guarantees space and existence for every competing stakeholder of life elements – individual, group, and institutional. These elements include social, political, economic and religious ideologies. Together they provide the basis for existence, power affiliation, growth, (scope for) achievement, and self-actualisation (Schein, 1994). Policies constitute the catalyst for the existence of each element.

The chapter also argued that policy implementation requires time within which it can be observed through individual, group, and institutional behaviour, in abidance with the stipulations of the policy, or in opposition to the policy's provisions. For that to happen, there must first and foremost be an abstract scenario during which the need to theoretically construct a compromise among competing desires is discussed, and instruments to monitor the levels of compliance are put in place. That is the role of administration – responding to social, political and economic challenges through policy initiatives (advocacy, debate and issuance of policy statements) – a manifestation of the abstract sphere. What follows is policy implementation, or the practical sphere, which in turn requires a clear work plan or programme that provides operational scope, structure and schedule. Both need space-demarcated areas within which execution of tasks and fulfilment of responsibilities can be easily observed, monitored, measured, quantified, and evaluated individually and collectively. That is the role of management – *working with and through people in the effort to achieve group or institutional objectives.*

It is anticipated that policy implementation is preceded by the gathering and analysis of data in an effort to understand the situation prompting the need for policy. As Case and Fair (1999, p. 364) put it:

> The role of policy makers is to understand the arguments, weigh the evidence, and proceed accordingly. While policy decisions must be made without knowledge of the outcome, enlightened uncertainty is better than ignorance.

Therefore, policies are initiated in response to a wide range of challenges. They should be implemented by an informed and trained team in order to ensure effectiveness and accomplishment of set goals and objectives. They should deliver through controlling human behaviour and ensuring the realisation of their extrinsic value – the social, political, and economic benefits they seek to provide to the community.

The scenarios discussed in this chapter put to rest what could be an opposing view – that policy process is a reaction to negative life experience. In actual fact, policy process can be a response to positive phenomena in society. It could be an effort to improve or maintain the good quality of services that a government is providing in the areas of education, health, security and food supply. The effort begins at the abstract level: are we satisfied with what we have? If not, what should we do? That does not mean that what is pertaining is all negative. Therefore, *the emergence of a policy marks the stakeholders' arrival at consensual agreement in terms of interpreting what is happening, and how the policy should be made to benefit society.* Competing arguments battle for supremacy during the agenda-setting debate. The perceptions, biases, contentions, and issues of legality are thoroughly analysed at that stage. Agenda issues set the tone of the policy process.

References

Anderson, J. E. (2003). *Public Policy Making.* (Fifth Edition) Boston: Houghton Mifflin.

Angula, N. & Bankie, B.F. (2000) (Eds). *The African Origin of Civilisation and the Destiny of Africa.* Windhoek: Gamsberg Macmillan.

Bayat, J-F. (1993). *The State in Africa – The Politics of the Belly.* London: Longman.

Beckman, P. R. (1984). *World Politics in the Twentieth Century.* Englewood Cliffs, NJ: Prentice Hall.

Blunt, P. & Jones, M. (1992). *Managing Organisations in Africa.* New York: Walter de Gruyter.

Case, K. E. & Fair, R. C. (1999). *Principles of Economics.* (Fifth Edition) Sydney: Prentice Hall of Australia.

DeLue, S. M. (1997). *Political Thinking, Political Theory, and Civil Society.* Singapore: Allyn and Bacon.

Fox, W., Schwella, E., & Wissink, H. (1991). *Public Management.* Cape Town: Juta.

Garang, J. (1994). A Speech on the Challenges of Political Liberation in Africa, made at the 7th Pan African Conference. Kampala, Uganda. April 1994.

Gibbon, P., Bangura, Y. & Ofstad, A. (1992) (Eds). *Authoritarianism, Democracy, and Adjustment – The Politics of Economic Reform in Africa.* Uppsala: Scandinavian Institute of African Studies.

Giddens, A. (1993). *Sociology.* (Second Edition) Oxford: Polity Press.

Glaucon's contribution to the debate on Socrates' City, quoted in Reeve, C. D. C. (1992). *Plato's Republic.* Indianapolis: Hackett Publishing.

Greenberg, J. & Baron, R. A. (2000). *Behaviour in Organisations: Understanding and Managing the Human Side of Work.* Englewood Cliffs, NJ: Prentice Hall.

Henry, N. (2001). *Public Administration and Public Affairs.* (Eighth Edition) Englewood Cliffs, NJ: Prentice Hall.

Hobbes quoted in Roskin, M. G., Cord, R. L., Medeiros, J. A. & Jones, W. S. (2000). *Political Science – An Introduction.* (Seventh Edition) Englewood Cliffs, NJ: Prentice Hall.

Lindblom, C. E. & Woodhouse, E. J. (1993). *Public Policy Making.* (Third Edition) Englewood Cliffs, NJ: PrenticeHall.

Maathai, Wangari (2009). Retrieved 19 January 2009, from http://en.wikipedia.org/wiki/wangari-maathai

Mad Mike & Mark (2008). Animal Planet TV Channel.

Malawi Decentralisation Secretariat (no date). Malawi Decentralisation Policy. Lilongwe: Government of Malawi.

Ministry of Education and Culture (MEC) (1993). The Language Policy for Schools 1992–1996 and Beyond. Windhoek: MEC.

Ministry of Regional and Local Government and Housing (MRLGH) (1998). Decentralisation in Namibia: The Policy, Its Development and Implementation. Windhoek: MRLGH.

Ministry of Youth, National Service, Sport and Culture (MYNSSC) (no date). National Youth Policy, Youth Growing with the Nation. Windhoek: MYNSSC.

Namibia: Epupa Dam Study, Kunene (1998). Retrieved 15 January 15 2009, from http:/www.africa.upenn.ed/Urgent_ Action/aspic.

National Food Security and Nutrition Council (NFSNC) (1995). Food and Nutrition Policy for Namibia. Windhoek: NFSNC.

National Planning Commission (NPC) (1997). National Population Policy for Sustainable Human Development. Windhoek: NPC.

National Planning Commission (NPC) (2004). Regional Planning and Development Policy. Windhoek: NPC.

National Society for Human Rights (NSHR) (no date). Assessing and Managing Environmental Impacts on Epupa Water Project in the Kunene Region of Namibia. Submission to the World Commission on Dams. Serial No. INS102. Windhoek: NSHR.

Parenti, M. (1978). *Power and the Powerless.* New York: St. Martin's Press.

Parker, C. (2003). *A Manual of Public Management.* Windhoek: Aim Publications.

Portes, A. (1998). Social Capital: its Origins and Applications in Contemporary Sociology. *Annual Review of Sociology* **24.**

Riots in Uganda (2007). Two Asians Dead, Temple Attacked. Retrieved 25 November 2008, from http://www.sepiamunity.com/sepia/archives/

Robbins, S. P. & Decenzo, D. A. (2004). *Fundamentals of Management. Essential Concepts and Applications.* (Fourth Edition) Englewood Cliffs, NJ: Pearson Prentice Hall.

Roskin, M. G., Cord, R. L., Medeiros, J. A. & Jones, W. S. (2000). *Political Science – An Introduction.* (Seventh Edition) Englewood Cliffs, NJ: Prentice Hall.

Schein, E. H. (1994). *Organizational Psychology.* (Third Edition) Englewood Cliffs, NJ: Prentice Hall.

Southern African Regional Institute for Policy Studies (1995). *Masters in Policy Studies – Research, Dialogue, Policy.* Harare: Southern Africa Printing and Publishing House.

United Nations Organisation (1992). *General Assembly Debates.* New York: United Nations.

Vansina, J. (1965). *Oral Traditions: A Study in Historical Methodology.* Chicago: Aldine Publishing.

Weatherby, J. N., Cruikshanks, R. L., Evans Jnr, E. B., Gooden, R., Huff, E. D., Kranzdorf, R., & Long, D. C. (2000). *The Other World.Issues and Politics of the Developing World.* (Fourth Edition) Sydney: Longman.

2

UNDERSTANDING THE SALIENT FORCES OF PUBLIC POLICY

Policies cement consensus on norms and values that characterise human behaviour and guarantee peaceful co-existence and developmental progress.

The world is awash with literature on policy-making processes depicting various views, focuses and objectives that put emphasis on a wide range of human life necessities and demands, manifesting in a mix of nature and its constituencies (Black *et al.* 2000; Case & Fair, 1999; Fox *et al.* 1991; Mondy *et al.* 1999; Otaala, 2003; Viotti & Kauppi, 2001). The processes are underpinned by complex salient forces, prompting Lindblom and Woodhouse (1993, p. 4) to state that:

> prior to politics, beneath it, enveloping it, restricting it,
> conditioning it, is the underlying consensus on policy that
> usually exists in the society among a predominant portion
> of the politically active members.

It should be added that all economic, educational and social activities that overtly seem to be apolitical, are unavoidably expressions of political decisions. As constituencies of human behaviour, policies about them link the past, the present, and the future, prompting Munroe (1997, pp. 81-93) to link leadership to the synergy between the needs and challenges of today and those of tomorrow. 'Wise leaders make choices that protect [their] vision, and vision should focus on change, demands and sacrifice,' he stated. That means that vision expresses the desire for a better tomorrow based on life qualities of today, as determined by the experiences of yesterday. Therefore, it is the past representing the dead, the present representing the living, and the future representing today's vision that could present joy or suffering for those yet to be born. These represent the three major theatres of policy causes, and each of these theatres hosts a myriad of cultural and developmental policy factors and linkages, as depicted in figure 3 on page 18.

Figure 3: Culture and Policy Developmental Perspectives

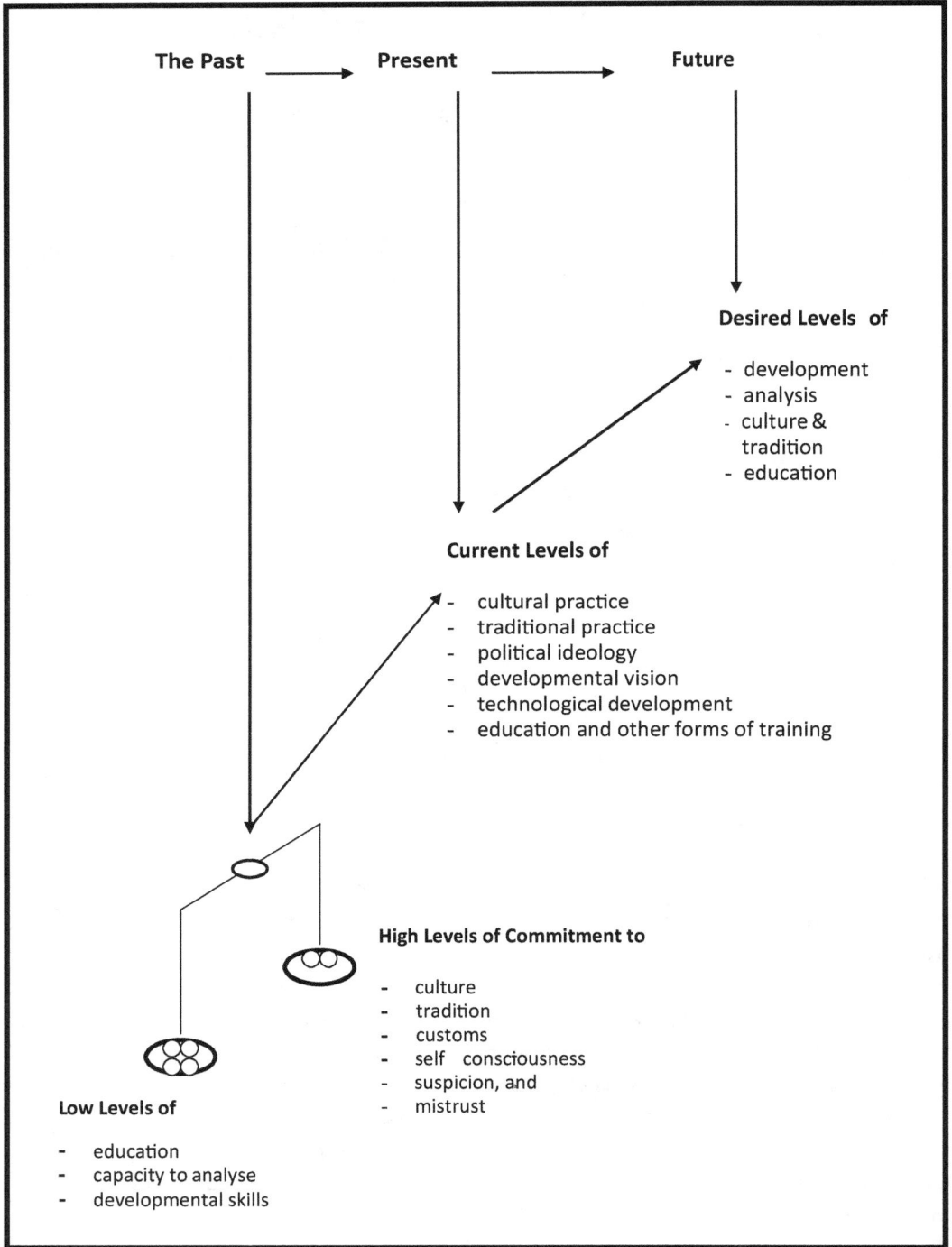

The Past ⟶ Present ⟶ Future

Desired Levels of

- development
- analysis
- culture &
  tradition
- education

Current Levels of

- cultural practice
- traditional practice
- political ideology
- developmental vision
- technological development
- education and other forms of training

High Levels of Commitment to

- culture
- tradition
- customs
- self consciousness
- suspicion, and
- mistrust

Low Levels of

- education
- capacity to analyse
- developmental skills

The Past Experience

Past policy processes were generally characterised by low levels of education, limited analytical skills, and impaired developmental vision, working in tandem with high levels of culture, tradition, self-consciousness, suspicion and mistrust, and an intensive sense of self-protection. Incontestably, education is and will continue to be the catalyst of psychological enlightenment, politically, socially and economically. It is also the key to understanding the 'trial and travail' of the early experience of human life. The huge strides in education, and our ability to analyse social, political and economic development, characterise current life experience. The readiness and capacity to utilise the gains in social, political, economic and educational development, in improving cultural and social practices, present a serious challenge to the values of past experience as they relate to the desired quality of life today and of tomorrow. The challenge beckons culture, tradition, and education to collaboratively produce a level of information developmentally concomitant with community views on policy issues. Human behaviour, as both a catalyst and a beneficiary of development, should be used as a single measure of policy output and outcome. It should link the qualities of the policies of yesteryear to the value of the current policy output, and seek to influence future policy designs portraying the human life experience continuum, explained through demographic as well as social, cultural, political, and economic factors that define the human life roller coaster.

With the exception of natural phenomena, human experience is largely a retrospection of the deeds of the dead that provide vital information on a wide range of policy issues concerning the whole world today. For example, ancient kingdoms and tombstones constitute a marvel of the past that the United Nations and countries of the world guard jealously. Without policies to protect them, their archaeological content, historical, and cultural value would vanish into thin air. The kingdoms, tombstones and other symbols depict the bond between the dead and the living, and between the past and the present. Even Hitler's wars – an experience of the past that connects the past, the present and the future in a continuous breath – are inseparable from the world's unity in the effort to prevent genocide.

However, the above discussion should not be misunderstood to mean that the present generation is in any way an inferior cause of policy. In fact it is the major cause, in that human beings hear, see, understand, analyse and reconstruct the past and the present experiences with the object of predicting and shaping a future they would like to have. Consequently, after analysing and understanding what they hear and see, they seek more information that can help them to make choices from every experience. As a result, academic knowledge, research and archaeology combine to inform present generations about ancestral achievements, thereby confirming the fact that it is the past that shaped the present. Africa's current demographic phenomena, cultural vibrancy, social interactions, political activities, and economic experiences are reminders of the Ghana, Mali, Songhai,

Monomutapa and Buganda kingdoms (to mention but a few), in which immigrations, migrations, cultural activities, politics and trade were the order of the day (Davison & Buab, 1996; Ajayi, 1978; Rotberg & Shore, 1988; Wilson & Thompson,1969; Uzoigwe, 1973).

What is important to note is that unless there are policies that govern human behaviour, there can be no order. That means disorder could be the order of the day if policies are robbed of their meaning: controlling human behaviour with the object of ensuring peaceful co-existence, and achieving sustainable incremental levels of development. That necessitates the need to retain past knowledge for the benefit of the present generation: there must be policies in place that encourage and protect the effort to preserve experiences of the past that laid the foundation of the present, whether good or bad. If the past was bad, corrections must be made. If it was good, it must be improved in order to keep pace with developmental strides taking place worldwide. The dead (who represent the past) constitute a major salient force of policy formulation because they are preserves of knowledge, cultural history and pride. They provide an identity dissimilar to any other. Hence, the necessity to protect cemeteries, tombs and shrines, historical ruins, petrified forests, and many other cultural artefacts or attestations of past life experience. It is from these that the present generations derive their identities, wisdom, and pride and, indeed, a meaningful source of life-inspiring behavioural control instruments – policies.

At the same time, the living are who they are because of the good and bad deeds of the dead, as well as their own good and bad deeds. By accepting and pronouncing historical legacies, the present generations must be mindful of man's fallibility. The errors of the past can be repeated if measures to prevent them are not put in place. However, progress in technology and education can assist in ensuring the non-repetition of undesirable history – a history that both present and the future generations cannot extricate themselves from as long as they are components of a chain that explains genealogical ties. In short, our ancestors had their ancestors, and we are destined to be ancestors. To that end, the ever-changing social, political, and economic environments characterise each generation. The changes signify new life-perceptions that in turn prompt appropriate behavioural controls in line with the prevailing understanding of what sustainable development means. At the same time, that does not necessarily mean doing away with every policy already in place. Instead, it further explains the relationship between the past and the present. Consequently, the present generation (the living) epitomises the same characteristics of the earlier generation and more:

- the need to preserve valued historical artefacts and phenomena;
- the necessity to ensure that peace and harmony prevail among different communities;
- the compulsion to support efforts aimed at providing life necessities of different types – food, shelter, clothing; and
- the duty to save the lives of unborn children and endangered species.

All these demand behavioural change by the present generation, and by more generations to come.

Policy making is, thus, a manifestation of synergies between vertical and horizontal interaction, and between norms and values working at differentiated societal and economic occupational levels (Guha, 1986), an output of social capital that Woolcock & Narayan (1987, p. 226) and Portes (1998, pp.1-24) refer to as *norms and networks that enable people to act collectively*. The focal point is the individual, representing eight social capital factors that provide the basis for citizens' involvement in policy formation (Woolcock & Narayan 1998; Anderson 2003). These social capital factors are:

1   participation in the local community;
2   pro-action in a social context;
3   feeling of trust and safety;
4   neighbourhood connections;
5   connections with family and friends;
6   tolerance of diversity;
7   recognition of the value of life; and
8   work connections (Woolcock & Narayan, 1998).

That said, *the broad aim of public policy is to serve the interests of as many people as possible and to satisfy as large a part of the society as possible* (Guha, 1986, p. 441; Portes, 1998, pp. 1-24). These views present two complementary situations necessary for a workable policy, namely 'strong intra-community' and 'weak inter-community' ties, that Gittel and Vidal (1998) refer to as bonding and bridging respectively. Simply put, an individual as the core element of both policy formation and policy consumption must contribute towards institutional ties that are exclusive to a limited group in all operational and functional aspects, e. g. a family, an extended family grouping, a tribe or an ethnic group. These are defined by their ethos, beliefs and practices that demand nothing less than total allegiance and obedience. Dissenters are jettisoned for bringing disrepute to the tightly organised group and closely followed norms. There is no doubt that each member is bonded to a group identity.

At the same time, meaningful survival demands elastic networking effective enough to provide those life requirements not necessarily found within a homogeneously exclusive community. For example, membership in a religious group, a football or netball club, or a professional organisation, comes with the acceptance of differences without being permanently bound to the objectives and mission of the organisation. One can choose to leave the group and suffer no serious consequences. It is different with family, tribe or ethnic membership, particularly within an African environment. Such membership enhances and indeed lubricates life fulfilment in that it recognises the importance of 'open' and 'human relations' systems that provide to the member the benefits necessary to make his/her life complete (Greenberg & Baron, 2000, pp. 5-15). In an African context, extended family ties within the same traditional grouping demonstrate the necessity and effectiveness of an open system. Family identities are upheld, but each is ever ready to come to the assistance of sister families in need, with the full knowledge that such help will be reciprocally provided when tables turn.

Bartering demonstrates yet another attestation of an open system at work. At the same time, recognition and respect for its contribution towards community social and economic needs, particularly in Africa, prove the omnipresence of 'human relations' system. The deserving individuals or communities are provided with the material needs or with empathy. Hence, it is the existence of the individual, and the quest to ensure his/her survival, that sets the primary compulsions for instruments that control behaviour. In the case of cultural and traditional norms and practices, policies are such instruments, although they are not necessarily written. An absence of behavioural control instruments could allow chaos to reign, as individual egos and competition for survival become everyone's preoccupation, with neither limitations nor recognition and respect of the fact that other community members also need to survive.

Given the above, it could be argued that policy is anchored in an individual's awareness of his/her own existence, which is largely dependent on important internal and external synergies and interventions. These include, among others:

- social formations focusing on economics, politics, religion, and the preservation of culture and tradition;
- the effects of geological and environmental properties – weather, fauna and flora, and topography;
- people as individuals, organisations or institutions; and
- arms of government as provided for by the constitution.

It is the extent to which each one of these factors influences or impacts on the individual that explains the relationship between the individual and policy as an instrument to control the individual's behaviour. To that end, the individual and the community must collaborate, and the environment must be an enabling one for any policy initiative to succeed. Neither one can be recognisable, exist, or contribute to the body of policy without the support and collaboration of the other two. This synergy implies that the existence of the individual conjures the necessity for policies that protect him/her from self-destruction and from destruction by external factors. This also applies to the community. At the same time, the individual and the community cannot exist without the external environment, which, in turn compels individuals and communities to protect it so that it can secure their future. That future is best explained by the need to ensure comprehensive security as articulated for all world communities in the Millennium Development Goals (MDGs), which guarantee sustainable provision of life necessities for both the living and those yet to be born. The individual, the community, and the environmentco-exist in a symbiotic relationship, and nurture each other somatically.

The scenario presents the individual as the smallest unit of a community that, in turn, is held together by common beliefs and practices representing a particular culture, and a particular tradition. That means that an individual's identity within a community is a manifestation of a relationship sustained by a set of behavioural commitments primarily entered into voluntarily, even though there is no other option. Yet nothing is written about the control measures, which are basically policies, generally referred to as norms and common practices. The question is, what then is a policy?

Policy 'gurus', who include J. E. Anderson (2003), R. E. Bovbjerg (1985), J. Dror (1968), S. X. Hanekom (1987), H. M. Ingram and J. E. Mann (1980), C. E. Lindblom (1968), G. A. Ojagbohunmi (1990), and O. S. Saasa (1985), among others, would concur that every policy seeks to control behaviour and the quality of the behavioural output, thereby making the policy *a regulatory intention setting operational specification aimed at achieving specific objectives beneficial to all citizenry through behavioural control.* This means the concept of policy begins by recognizing behaviour as the basis of life, which should be supported and protected by instruments that society needs, in order to attain sustainable and peaceful future life satisfaction.

Implications

The above definition has four important implications.

First, that *policy is a process embedded in individual, institutional or government initiatives emerging out of phenomenal linkages in every community, society or nation.* The causes are many, given the fact that national survival depends on various social political, economic, and environmental activities: how the citizens are protected, or provided with goods and services; how much political freedom the citizens enjoy; and the extent to which the environment enables the citizens to generate own income, or enables business enterprises to create jobs through expansion of their income-generating initiatives. These imply that harmonious synergy is required in order to ensure that the country's borders are secured; political culture is encouraged and sustained; communication is not only constructed and maintained, but is continuously improved; roads are constructed; houses are built; clothes are manufactured; food is processed; and economic activities are supported and subsidised if necessary. How this is done requires behavioural control instruments that guarantee consistency in terms of the tasks' output, and ensure equity regarding gender and constituency representation. In addition, the delivery and receipt of the goods and services should be reliable.

Second, the relevance of policy implies that the individual who is a policy consumer must exist first before he/she behaviourally plays a role in society. That existence is guaranteed by institutional control measures designed to ensure the individual's security in terms of social, political and economic rights. These are important to maintain life. Hence, there are some policies against abortion and possible parental negligence to meet child care obligations. It is indeed a collective vision of world governments, in particular the United Nations, to preserve human life through a wide range of programmes. As a result, the existence of one entails the existence of one plus one – the community in a society, in which interdependence is the catalyst for individual and collective survival.

Third, the flourishing of trust and respect between government and the citizens, and among the citizens themselves, is a sign of recognition of the existence of each other as individuals, of national political authority, and the constituencies and membership it represents. In fact, it is a sign of peaceful co-existence among the citizens and their institutions. An absence of these means the absence of necessary cross-cutting synergy that provides peace and harmony in society. The scenario entails continuity of life-saving activities of a specific nature and scope at different levels; a relationship between policies as institutional behavioural control measures, and the individual policy implementers, beneficiaries and targets of such measures; and continuous decision making in an unending sequence of activities designed to control human behaviour within the constituencies of societal organisational stratifications that host and characterise the policy making process.

Fourth, intra-community ties provide the policy maker with not just 'a sense of identity and common purpose but also with a social, political and economic base' (Astone *et al.* 1999, quoted in Woolcock & Narayan, 2000, p. 230). This was best demonstrated by Zimbabwe's former political critic who turned into the government's voice (the Minister of Information), only to fall out with the president a short time later, and who went on to win a parliamentary seat in the 2004 general election as an independent candidate. He was a beneficiary of policies that he, as Minister, initiated to benefit his home base, exemplifying 'strong intra-community ties' (Woolcock & Narayan 2000, p. 230).

Intra-community Levels

The influence of intra-community ties manifests at two levels. First, it occurs:

1   during the resultant debates characterising the agenda-setting stage (the sifting of the arguments around each idea or issue competing to be put on the policy agenda);
2   during the processing of the issue once it has been put on the policy agenda (determining with certainty the impact of each issue and who the affected people and other stakeholders are); and

3   during the consideration of the options (prioritising possible levels of response and providing convincing motivation) (Fox *et al.* 1991).

It becomes a direct involvement in which a policy maker parrots constituent concerns hiding behind national generic needs for improving human security. That means maximum provision of social, political and economic needs. At the same time any possible but undesirable interventions: illiteracy, unemployment, poverty, disease and crime should be prevented. Whereas the arguments each participant in the policy debate puts forward propagate popular demand, in actual fact they constitute a hidden strategy to push a personal agenda through the best means available, thereby demonstrating Thomas Hobbes' statement that 'The power of man is his present means to obtain some future apparent good' (Parenti, 1978, p. 4).

Second, intra-community ties also benefit the community through effective implementation of policies that are already on the books. He who needs community favours and support should do for it what it cannot do for itself. That means spearheading the implementation of government policies that are on the books but not implemented. Only an insider can do that. It, thus, becomes the responsibility of the policy maker to identify policies that stand a good chance of being implemented in his/her community. The effort should be accompanied by realistic capacity for making the needed action realisable. Therefore, the necessary inputs must be assembled in recognition of the fact that *'socio-political power is not [only] self-generated but [is] acquired through the attachments of many individual energies, strengths, and talents to one or a few wills'* (Parenti, 1978, p. 7; my italics). This lends credence to the communitarian perspective that 'sound capita-norms and networks that enable people to act collectively – is inherently good, that more is better, and that its presence always has a positive effect on a community's welfare' (Woolcock, 1998, p. 151). Simply put, a policy maker can identify with a community in a way that yields mutual benefits as a result of his/her individual initiative, and can also identify with the community through spearheading the implementation of policies formulated by others who were not affected.

The total result of the symbiosis is that the individual needs the community through which to exhibit policy related skills and functions, and the community needs individuals' confederacy action in the form of a consensual code of behaviour that puts limitations on individual choices in preference of majority interests. Arrival at a consensus on the code of behaviour always guarantees peaceful co-existence. It also brings about the realisation of social, political, and economic needs brought about and sustained by policies that are formulated, implemented, and evaluated through organisational structures. Therefore, the primacy of the individual, in particular his needs to survive, compels those interested in understanding the role of public policy in national development, and those involved in the policy process, to take heed of DeLue's views that:

> In the public realm, individuals interact with each other to purchase or sell goods, to make a living, or to help make public policies. To be sure, the nature of the public/private dichotomy is such that individuals must be governed, no matter what their private values may be, by common public norms that are applicable to all citizens. In a civil society, accepting common norms means that all must respect the rights of all other citizens. Owing to this commitment, then, persons must accept limits on how far they can press their private values in the public realm (1997, p. 313).

However, the need to satisfy personal desires, interests and values precedes the scenario of purchasing and selling goods to make a living, and participation in making public policy. The quest to make a living manifests through interaction among members of the society. Such interaction explains the inadequacy of an individual's capacity to provide all of the life necessities for him/herself. As a result, a communal environment is needed that provokes and encourages developmental creativity within the limits that foster consensus on forms of behaviour. Every community must first and foremost be at peace with itself – the members must accept the limits on how far they can press their private interests (values) without violating other citizen's rights and causing conflict. Consequently, accepted policies are the only guarantor for a community to be at peace with itself, provided the external environment is a cooperating partner.

We take cognisance of the primacy of the individual in every policy process, in that the individual must first and foremost be conscious not only of his/her existence (who he/she is), but must also respect the existence of the other community members because they provide collective assistance to the community in various ways. However, it should also be recognised that community members provide friendship, security, and different types of support (for example, in areas of employment, education, and in times of death) to each and every individual within the group. Consequently, the individual is obliged to reciprocate in those relationships, based on the quest to survive – itself a battle that cannot be won unless the rights of others are recognised. Hence, those relationships should be respected and not violated through intentional behavioural acts. That can only be achieved through application of 'necessita: the limitations placed upon human choice by the society in which political decisions must be made' (Johnson, 1966, p. 89).

As Parenti (1978, p. 8) correctly states, 'individuals have been known to pursue political goals for other than egotistic gain, that is, for ethical ideological reasons.' That means that in the absence of behavioural control measures such as policies, other people who are conscious of their ability to use whatever means at their disposal to get what they want could do so without hesitation. Therefore, policy process begins with the individual's quest to survive in an environment in which social and economic resources on the one side, and greed and poverty on the other, co-exist in equal abundance. The challenge is how best to balance the utilisation of the resources and the consumption thereof in the midst of constant conflict between economic opulence and social destitution. Policies seek to achieve that balance through behavioural control. That means that citizens, acting as members of society, have their own individual compelling social, political and economic needs that impact on the community's ability to provide. Given the inequalities in every society, the supply of needed goods and services would manifest in an undesirably uneven manner were it not for policies that government puts in place. Even networking among the citizens and among organisations has difficulty equitably involving those who are stuck at the low levels of the national economic ladder, because most of them lack the skills and capacity to be effective participants. Policies uplift their spirits and oblige the privileged to involve the weak in the activities to create and provide social and economic necessities. Policies also seek to bridge the gap between the 'haves' and the 'have nots'. It is a challenge which is difficult, if not impossible, to win, and one that means that policy making continuously responds to changing life demands dictated by dichotomous causes – social, political, and economic disparities.

Conclusion

This chapter stressed that life is the primary salient force of policy. Consequently, there is a need for a conscious and, indeed, concerted effort to improve the policy process in order to nurture, sustain, and protect life. The chapter highlighted the synergies between the past and the present, and between the present and the envisaged future. Whereas life gives birth to behaviour manifesting through people, the behaviour results in actions that compel policy demands and action. As a result, past actions largely become the basis of present actions and that, in turn, suggests what must be done for the sake of tomorrow. The actions' quantum focuses on the need to facilitate, improve, nurture, and sustain life progressively and qualitatively, such that future generations are not in any way disadvantaged.

The chapter also discussed the imperatives and value of inter- and intra-community social formations, underlining the fact that life begins at the nuclear family level. However, an individual needs symbiotic relations with members of a broader community in order to sustain him/herself (achieve longevity). Not to accept that reality would suggest that an individual is fully self-sufficient, and that is not possible. Therefore, it is necessary to have policies that regulate the synergies and symbioses among the variables that constitute the units of human life, so as to ensure equitable production as well as delivery and receipt of goods and services that guarantee the continuity of life. Furthermore, the chapter emphasised the necessity to understand the compulsions of age and personal interests. These underpin human behaviour. They make up the driving force behind every human initiative or reaction to policy challenges of all kinds. It was also argued that the bond between the dead and the living is permanent; and that the intra- and inter-community bonds that explain human relations within communities, as well as the societal needs constitute the major salient forces that coherently drive the policy process.

References

Ajayi, J. F. A. (1978) (Ed.). *A History of West Africa.*Volume Two. Aylesbury, UK: Hazell Watson & Viney.

Anderson, J. E. (2003). *Public Policy Making.* (Fifth Edition) Boston: Houghton Mifflin Company, Inc.

Astone, N. M., Nathanson, C., Schoen, C. A., Young, R. & Kim, J. K. (1999). Family Demography, Social Theory, and Investment in Social Capital. *Population and Development Review* **25**(1).

Black, P., Hartzenberg, T. & Standish, B. (2000). *Economic Principles and Practice.* (Second Edition). Cape Town: Cape Town Graduate School of Business.

Bovbjerg, R. E. (1985). What is Policy Analysis? *Journal of Policy Analysis and Management* **5**(1).

Case, K. E. & Fair, R. C. (1999). *Principles of Economics.* (Fifth Edition). Sydney: Prentice Hall of Australia.

Davison, B. & Buab, F. K. (1966). *A History of West Africa to The Nineteenth Century.* New York: Doubleday.

DeLue, S. M. (1997). *Political Thinking, Political Theory, and Civil Society.* Singapore: Allyn and Bacon.

Dror, J. (1968). *Public Policy-making Re-examined.* New York: American Elsevier.

Dunn, W. N. (1981). *Public Policy Analysis: An Introduction.* Englewood Cliffs, NJ: Prentice Hall.

Fox, W., Schwella, E. & Wissink, H. (1991). *Public Management.* Cape Town: Juta.

Giddens, A. (1993). *Sociology.* (Second Edition) Oxford: Polity Press.

Gittel, R. & Vidal, A. (1998). *Community Organising: Building Social Capital as a Development Strategy.* Newbury Park, California: Sage Publications.

Greenberg, J. & Baron, R. (2000). *Behaviour in Organisations: Understanding and Managing the Human Side of Work.* Englewood Cliffs, NJ: Prentice Hall.

Guha, A. (1986). An Alternative Approach to Public Policy. *International Social Science Journal.*XXXVIII (109).

Hanekom, S. X. (1987). *Public Policy: Framework and Instrument for Action.* Johannesburg: Macmillan.

Ingram, H. M. & Mann, J. E. (1980). *Why Policies Succeed or Fail.* Beverley Hills, California: Sage.

Johnson, C. (1996). *Revolutionary Change.* Boston: Little, Brown and Company.

Lindblom, C. E. (1968). *The Policy-Making Process.* Englewood Cliffs, NJ : Prentice- Hall.

Lindblom, C. E. & Woodhouse, E. J. (1993). *Public Policy Making.* (Third Edition) Englewood Cliffs, NJ: Prentice Hall.

Mondy, R. W., Noe, R. M. & Premeaux, S. R. (1999). *Human Resources Management.* (Seventh Edition) Englewood Cliffs, NJ: Prentice Hall.

Munroe, M. (1992). *In Pursuit of Purpose.* Shippensburg, PA: Destiny Image Publishers.

Ojagbohunmi, G. A. (1990). Institutionalisation of Policy Analysis in Developing Countries with Special Reference to Nigeria. *Working Paper Series* No. 83. The Hague: Institute of Social Studies.

Otaala, B. (2003) (Ed.). *HIV/AIDS – Government Leaders in Namibia Responding to the HIV/AIDS Epidemic.* Windhoek: University of Namibia Press.

Parenti, M. (1978). *Power and the Powerless.* New York: St. Martin's Press.

Portes, A. (1998). Social Capital: its Origins and Applications in Contemporary Sociology. *Annual Review of Sociology* **24.**

Roskin, M. G. & Berry, N. O. (1999). *The New World of International Relations.* (Fourth Edition) Englewood Cliffs, NJ: Prentice Hall.

Roskin, M. G., Cord, R. L., Medeiros, J. A., & Jones, W. S. (2000). *Political Science – An Introduction* (Seventh Edition) Englewood Cliffs, NJ: Prentice Hall.

Rotberg, R. I. & Shore, M. F. (1988). *The Founder, Cecil Rhodes and the Pursuit of Power.* Johannesburg: Southern Book Publishers.

Saasa, O. S. (1985). Public Policy Making in Developing Countries. The Utility of Contemporary Decision Making Models. *Public Administration and Development* **5**(4).

Uzoigwe, G. N. (1973) (Ed.). *Anatomy of an African Kingdom. A History of Bunyoro-Kitara.* New York: NOK Publishers.

Viotti, P. R. & Kauppi, M. V. (2001). *International Relations and World Politics, Security, Economy, Identity.* Second Edition. Englewood Cliffs, NJ: Prentice Hall.

Wilson, M. & Thompson, L. (1969) (Eds). *The Oxford History of South Africa.* London: Oxford University Press.

Woolcock, M. (1998). Social Capital and Economic Development: Towards a Theoretical Synthesis and Policy Framework. *Theory and Society* **27**(2).

Woolcock, M. & Narayan, D. (2000). Social Capital: Implications for Development Theory, Research and Policy. *The World Bank Research Observer* **15**(2).

3

LIFE FACTORS AND POLICY PROCESS

For it to be viable, policy should be anchored in the confluence of diverse opinions that epitomise the dynamics and challenges of life in society.

Every human act is either caused or initiated. Policies are no different. Experience has demonstrated that there are specific life factors within which policy processes manifest. These are society, national and local politics, personal views, public and private sector activities, and external factors.

Societal Factors

Society is an embodiment of a multiplicity of environments, contentious issues, and competing egos. Human behaviour is generally the common bond among them, in that it provides the measurement of individual and collective (family, community or society) reaction to life challenges. Environmentally, society experiences *natural phenomena* in the form of disasters, floods, drought and earthquakes. The effects of each dictate societal reaction and citizens' behaviour. Naturally, expectation necessitates a state of readiness, *vis-à-vis* organisational preparedness to respond timeously and qualitatively to these phenomena.

Social environment

The social environment, such as natural socialisation among people, poses policy demands in areas of education, health, recreation and entertainment, to mention but a few. Each of these has its own policy requirements. For example *health* services entail policies on the recruitment of qualified personnel to specific positions that only people who have undergone special training should occupy; doctors with particular specialisations, nurses, radiographers, technicians, pharmacists, and managers of theatres and intensive-care units, are some of them. Education, recreation and entertainment, as well as housing, focus on specific policy areas.

Cultural environment

The cultural environment is another policy habitat that hosts several policy challenges.

Cultural identity, practice, and norms inculcate in members a uniform mentality and behaviour supported by common psychological beliefs that influence their perceptions about life in general. More often than not, cultural groupings comprise several subcultures that conscientiously accept the superiority of the main culture. These phenomena make culture a manifestation of peaceful co-existence of diverse sub-groups. Sustenance of the harmony among them requires policy instruments designed specifically to control behaviour. Cultural policies are largely unwritten.

Political environment

Additionally, the political environment poses its own policy challenges. It goes without saying that everything that happens in a country, be it action or inaction, occurs due to the presence, absence, implementation, or non-implementation of public policies. In other words, government tolerates civil society and private sector policy initiatives if the initiatives do not seem to threaten peace and tranquillity, and ignores them if their initiatives encourage economic development without necessarily causing policy problems. Furthermore, the political environment combines internal and external factors of human security. These include reliable and consistent provision of goods and services that guarantee human security. In order to successfully achieve that goal, individuals, communities, non-governmental organisations, and governments must be involved in the policy process.

Economic environment

It is important to note that the economic environment plays a critical role in every successful policy process. Government's ability to continuously and reliably deliver goods and services at national, regional and local levels, is supported by the ability of the private and informal sectors, and depends on the vibrancy of the economic environment which, in turn, is made possible by (good) policies. Issues of available natural resources, human resources, trade agreements with other countries, local capacity building programmes, good management of demographic dynamics in terms of skills, standard of living, and foreign direct investments, characterise the economic environment. The impact of each on society depends on its operational effectiveness, given the fact that there are ever-competing and, indeed, growing interests manifesting in a complex web of incessant consumer demands, and unending defiance of rules and regulations by some sectors of the society and economy.

Society mirrors struggles for existence and dominance in a fractious collectivity 'where people (or animals) suffer or prosper for reasons unconnected with ethical merit – for being ugly or beautiful respectively' (Orwell, 1946, p. x). This is because societies are a multiplicity of distinct groupings, communities, regions, political ideologies, cultural beliefs and practices, traditions and social-economic classes. The purpose, qualities, and characteristics of each variable exhibit the individuality and/or exclusivity of personal or organisational definitions of the situation at hand. Given the mobility of society and the dynamism of nature, 'we are always moving from one situation to another, and how we react, what our motives will be, will depend largely on how we define or structure that situation' (Schein, 1994, p. 41). The process of structuring a given situation is done not necessarily as an act of ridicule or adjuring stakeholders to challenge authority, but as an (albeit instinctive) manifestation of Maslow's hierarchy of motivational dictates, namely, *physiological needs; safety needs; affiliation, love and social needs; self-esteem needs;* and *self-actualisation* (Schein, 1994). At the same time, care must be taken, because the exclusivity of personal or organisational activities could deprive other people and some organisations' of their rights. It is here where it becomes necessary to have policy that legalises or legitimises the actions of one without violating the rights of others.

Therefore, society is a habitat of a multiplicity of interests and egos. Each strives for independent survival and recognition of its collective constitutional rights. As a result, each fiercely challenges for eminence in the policy process. Hence, society presents a force of individual traditions that cannot be ignored because people, families and communities make up tradition through consensual practice and agreement on the values they attach to each and every activity or symbol, in spite of internal differences. Consequently, political ideologies cannot be overlooked, because the basis and support of each ideology represents a society as a diverse grouping of people within which interests, egos, and various other elements of life are in constant competition. Unless actions are guided, monitored and controlled, each has a potential to destroy the others, and eventually to self-destruct. That, indeed, makes society the main factor of the policy process.

As already discussed in the preceding chapters, society maintains its structure through broad consensus among its members, who realise and accept the permanency of differences among them and, at the same time, agree to shoulder the cost in order to co-exist in peace as a primary condition for nurturing the identity of each member and of the collectivity – the society as a whole. It is a condition caused by written and unwritten policies, enforced by rules and regulations, which every member of the society should abide by if he/she wants to avoid being ostracised. At the same time, it should be recognised that it is human nature to serve one's own interests first before attending to those of others. Simply put, people are naturally biased and selfish due to the limited resources that are (always) unevenly distributed in the community. Policies are, thus, tools designed to create and maintain harmony and equity in a fractious society. Yet, as Parenti (1978, p. 181) observed:

> The policies of government are made in the name of society itself but policy outputs commonly serve partial or special interests rather than universal ones, their costs and benefits rarely reaching everyone with equal effect.

Consequently, government policy processes reflect societal scenarios in which the stakeholders realise the importance of co-existence and, at the same time, tirelessly work for their group and/or personal interests. The policies serve to regulate group and individual behaviour, but they are often violated if and when abidance comes into direct conflict with the interests and practice of the dominant group, or personal economic choices. That confirms the view that human beings live in a complex society (Roskin *et al.* 2000), in which policies should be continuously evaluated because their costs and benefits rarely reach everyone with equal effect.

It could be argued that policy aims to mitigate the intensity and in many cases vagrancy of bonded and bridged interests among members of society situationally subjected to vengeance, jealousy, hatred, corruption, political agendas and genuine expression of patriotic ideas. These largely influence the constituencies of the policy process. They also generate positional and ideological rivalries that characterise institutional politics over the promotion of values.

Danziger (2001, p. 4) defined such politics as 'the process through which power and influence are used in the promotion of certain values and interests…at many levels: individual, group and societal'. Many other definitions abound. The definitions fall into two categories, namely high politics concerned with war and peace, and low politics focusing on economic or environmental issues (Hughes, 2000, p. 33). Therefore, politics make society a vibrant sector during policy process. It merits that recognition in two ways.

First, politics itself is an instrument for policy making because it is used to promote the views that each and every policy stakeholder would like to hear or see discussed. Its use includes wooing of neutrals in the battle to thwart the opposition, thereby making the policy that ultimately emerges a direct product of political machination (intrigue).

Second, 'all politics is a struggle for power' (Morgenthau, quoted in Roskin *et al.* 2000, p. 23). It once more underpins Thomas Hobbes' view that 'The power of man is his present means to obtain some future apparent "good", whether it be morally good is not considered' (Parenti, 1978, p. 4). This point of view strongly suggests that there should be policies to control the business of promoting own views and interests, or the powerless will be forever doomed. It means that politics also need 'policy controls' at local, regional, and national levels. *Political office bearers must operate within given and clearly stipulated policy parameters, and must operationalise policies to their fullest extent, even in the circumstances where the policy objectives work against the office bearers' egos, interests, and cultural beliefs.* If implemented with an emphasis on the need for society to have a vibrant middle class, a government with a good administration, and democracy, the process would support Aristotle's political argument in the following quotation.

> The best political community is formed by citizens of the middle class, and those states are likely to be well administered in which the middle class is large, in which the citizens have moderate and sufficient property; for where some possess much and others nothing there may arise an extreme democracy or a pure oligarchy, or a tyranny may develop out of either extremes... Democracies are safer and more permanent than oligarchies, because they have a middle class which is more numerous and has a greater share in government, for when there is no middle class, and the poor greatly exceed in number, troubles arise, and the state soon comes to an end (Roskin *et al.* 2000, p. 21).

Auguste Comte, David Easton, and Hegel propagated 'behavioural', 'systems', and 'developmentalist' theories (see Roskin *et al.* 2000), which respectively proffer the view that policies are in fact, outputs of political games prompted by humankind's quest to maximise pleasure, achieved only through a consensus among the community members, using an institution that consultatively and acceptably regulates and promotes the public good. DeLue (1997, p. 125) refers to such institutional policy mandate as 'the most distinguishing feature of political authority [with] powers far wider and its coercive abilities to ensure compliance far more extensive'. Furthermore, policies are formulated to mitigate disparities in society which, as Vansina (1965) puts it, is the operative factor in deciding upon the significance of events.

National and Local Politics

In addition to constituting a policy environment, the political factor is all-embracing, because politics is about governance, an embedment of rules and regulations, most importantly policies. It is a 'culture [consisting] of citizens' beliefs and attitudes about government, authority, and political participation' (Weatherby *et al.* 2000, p. 80). Preceding political culture is people's agreement to live together in peace and harmony: arrival at a 'social contract – individuals joining and staying in civil society [associations between families and government]' (Rousseau, quoted in Roskin *et al.* 2000, p. 23). The development is a manifestation of a sense of belonging to a collectivity living in an environment largely made up of compromises, prompting rules and regulations for both government and the civil society. Each must accept the views and interests of the other in order for harmony to prevail within the community. Hence, politics become 'the process through which power and influence are used in the promotion of certain values and interests' (Danziger, 2001, p. 4). Policy plays a balancing act by providing behavioural parameters or control mechanisms designed to foster commitment to the security of all, through prevention of harm to any member, in a win–win situation managed and enforced by government institutions. This happens at both national and local levels.

Personal Views

In the view of one HIV/AIDS victim and activist, 'Policy-makers tend to pretend to know and understand our needs and therefore develop policies without our involvement, but such policies do not meet our needs and demands' (Martin, 2007).

Although not an environment by definition, *personal views* constitute a policy factor that is pivotal to every policy process. They engender the experiences of individuals, and of shared community values in the form of different cultural and traditional beliefs and practices, community and/or local politics, environmental pressures, individual and collective economic needs, common developmental demands, and specific life experiences. All of these are pivotal to the policy process because individuals are always concerned with their own welfare first before they pay attention to the welfare of others. Normally, they want to see that state organs and private sector institutions promote fair play across the board because 'relations between and among individuals can be unfair or unequal if the power that individuals can exercise [either through states or markets] is unequally distributed' (Alexander Hamilton, quoted in Balaam & Veseth, 2001, p. 15). Personal views, thus, play an important role in the success or failure of policy process. They are key building blocks of every policy process, in that they constitute the smallest units of policy beneficence.

Personal views are also indicators of particular life requirements in an explanatory relationship between an individual and the other community members at different levels. The views manifest in the realm of historicity – 'an outlook in which knowledge of social processes is used to reshape the social conditions of our existence' (Giddens, 1993, p. 645), thereby amplifying Emile Durkheim's first principle of sociology: '[the] study [of] social facts as things' (quoted by Giddens). Thomas Hobbes and Jean-Jacques Rousseau argued that in so doing people seek to improve their social well-being as a 'naturally perverse and destructive lot or as noble savages – spontaneous, outgoing, loving, kind and peaceful' (Zanden, 1990, p. 221). At the same time, people as individuals and communities hold different views about the nature of both social facts and things. Coupled with the necessity to improve lives in one way or another, the views people hold are those determined by how they perceive and interpret the situation impacting on them at present. Inasmuch as the views bounce off the prevailing situation, they also represent the thinking of those affected, particularly in terms of what to do about the situation, and what specific action to take. In other words, *life-quality is a product of controlled human behaviour in areas of knowledge: how to acquire and use knowledge with regards to the production and provision of goods and services, and how to evaluate the overall policy process – determining the necessity, adequacy, appropriateness, effectiveness, acceptability, implementability, value, and the use of knowledge built thereon.* It would be utopia to think people could arrive at a total national consensus on any one of these. Therefore, every policy has opposition.

It should also be noted that societies are complex and that they represent a wide range of areas of contention and conflict, and several levels of social formation, classification, and literacy, as well as various local and regional groupings, representing a rainbow of political orientations. The complexity depicts a diversity of opinions and views on facts and things that mirror human endeavours to achieve psychological and/or material needs that ensure personal growth and justify self-actualisation. It all points to the fact that everything that human beings do stems from our perception and interpretation of the environment and the situations we find ourselves in, and what we want to do about them. Therefore, whatever we decide to do entails action based on behavioural change as a direct response to situational dictates. It requires policy to achieve what we want.

This point conjures the necessity to look at policy formation through the eyes of the policy formulator. Having argued earlier that society is complex and is, indeed, rife with contentious issues and rivalries of different types, it would signal serious naivety to expect genuine positional neutrality during policy process. At the same time, outright honesty in expressing the reasons for taking particular positions, or for supporting positions other than those that align one with specific communities or broad groups in exchange for future reciprocity, is anathema to the social bonding (strong intra-community ties) and bridging (weak but important inter-community ties) referred to earlier.

Granovetter (1995) argued that these ties are intrinsically valuable because they allow individuals to initially draw on the benefits that close community membership provides, and enable them to acquire skills, resources, and fellowship resulting from broad networking that transcends nucleus or extended family boundaries (Woolcock & Narayan, 2000). Put differently, an individual participating in formulating policies that are likely to have a direct or indirect impact on him/her does so discreetly: making sure that what he/she says first and foremost seeks to enhance the benefits that accrue to him/her, and does so hiding behind public interest issues as a stratagem to ensure acceptance of a disguised personal agenda by the other members involved. Phrases such as 'people', 'the country', 'the community', and 'our people' become the daily linguistic recipe, basically using others to get ahead the Machiavellian way (Greenberg & Baron, 2000; Roskin *et al.* 2000).

Blat, a Russian informal network of complicity that managers enter into as a means of assuring that their organisational goals are met, explains success as a result of pushing for an acceptance of personal policy views through individualism disguised as collectivism, and 'is characterised by a high degree of mutual, almost familial trust' among those participating in the debate. Sometimes they are 'willing to enter into illicit deals with one another' in order to ensure that the idea is accepted and implemented (Henry, 2001, pp. 120-1). It is all done under a gentleman's agreement that virtually guarantees future reciprocal support. In short, policy formulation brings high quality stratagems out of the individual participants, and those stratagems articulate and seek implementation of selfish views through public national agenda programmes that project government's commitment to serve the citizenry. Whatever the outcome of the policy may be, personal views provide the recipe.

Private Sector

> It is not the benevolence of the butcher, the brewer, or the baker that we expect our dinner, but from their regard of their own interest. We address ourselves, not to their humanity but to their self-love, and never talk to them of our own necessities, but of their advantages (Smith, 1994).

The private sector is committed to profit; hence, it strives to make more and more profit. Therefore, given the large amounts of tax that it pays annually, it expects government to create an economically enabling environment. However, things do not always happen that way. Consequently, the private sector is forced to take whatever action is necessary to ensure that sufficient numbers of people sympathetic to its vision, mission, and economic objectives, are elected to parliament. To that end, it becomes unavoidable for the private sector to indirectly sponsor or support political aspirants during presidential, parliamentary and council elections, because it would be the height of political absurdity for the private sector itself to form a political party. In fact, it would be economic suicide to do so. All they can do is identify and support those candidates known to sympathise with the profit motive that characterises the private sector as a major factor of the policy process. This is a world-wide phenomenon.

Among the reasons that make private-sector-sponsored candidates succeed, are financial support for their campaign, loud pronouncements by private sector companies that they will retrench workers if government fails to meet them halfway, and the high price put on continued prospective employment of voters in large numbers. Every government is very aware of the fact that it will lose support, particularly voters, in the event that the private sector fires or retrenches large numbers of employees. These are general and common sense facts that need no citation.

Important to note is the fact that the private (business and commercial) sector constitutes very strong interests characteristically similar to those of social and political groupings. Unless government creates an environment that encourages and supports business, the latter will constitute something of a rival system to the public policy making process, garnering support from the masses who always want jobs, most of which are provided by the private sector. As a result, the private or business sector circumstantially and indirectly involves itself in policy making. It does so through lobbying, resisting government policy prescriptions if they are not conducive to profit making, and by funding election campaigns of candidates viewed to be supportive of business (Lindblom & Woodhouse, 1993). This is done in order to ensure the survival of the self, as an individual or organisation. When done collectively, oligopoly (a conspiracy among members of the private sector in the same business to undermine genuine competition) usually takes over, and shapes the private sector's views on national policy, particularly those on economics, trade, and labour issues.

Therefore, society as a complex and, indeed, indivisible embedment of a common social, political and economic position, and as an indicator of service and material needs, presents issues that demand policy attention. At the same time, the complexity of society manifests through a rainbow of social and political formations, each with its own policy demands that need to be addressed, sometimes independently, thereby requiring effective representation at all policy making fora. As to the nature of representation, the personal views of the participants in the policy debate have to be taken into account. After all, it is the ability of each participant to convince his/her colleagues during the debates to make the decision that he/she wants to see made – the decision that reflects his/her views. Such views invariably reflect cultural beliefs and practices, and personal understanding and interpretation of the environment – factors influencing relationships among the life variables – such as politics and economics.

> After all, if we are to understand what a person is doing
> in a given situation and why, we must seek to understand
> the person's definition of the situation (Schein, 1994, p. 41).

Given the seemingly omnipresent interdependence among people; between people and organisations; between people and government; and between people and their environment, the impact and influence of the external forces on policy formulation is a guaranteed phenomenon. However, external forces are not homogeneous; each has its own orientation that projects a distinct view on events and policy priorities. The lack of homogeneity unavoidably presents two constituencies of external forces, namely external to the country, and external to the organisation but manifesting within the same country. At the same time, geographic differences come with distinct priorities of their own that are important to the overall policy debate output – the scope of the policy programme/activities – determining the objective, inputs, operational parameters, and overall networking. As a result, it is necessary to put in place behavioural mechanisms that control the actions of both individuals and other stakeholders, so as to ensure their procedural and possibly collaborative involvement in the policy process. However, continuous life challenges in the form of population growth, labour migration, increasing levels of literacy, technological advances, inflation, and political instability, will continue to put pressure on policy costs, implementability, acceptability, and relevance. Consequently, these phenomena bind the private sector to government initiatives to provide policy solutions that seek to achieve national development, even if this is done grudgingly.

External Sector

As increased regional, continental, and intercontinental trade continues to reduce the world community to a global village, we might assume that the occurrence of conflict will be curbed. However, reality provides contrary experiences. The world is still a beehive of insecurity and conflicts, which conjure concerted efforts to find lasting solutions. The gap between the developed and the developing countries in terms of the creation and use of technology is also prompting control measures in the case of manufacturing war material, and in increasing the levels of education and training in order to acquire and use technology for further development. Therefore, it is necessary to discuss the two sets of *external forces* contextually.

Having admittedly conceded that policy making is embedded in politics (Ministry of Regional and Local Government and Housing, 1998; Mawhood, 1993; Jordaan, 2001; Fox *et al.* 1991; Cloete, *et al.* 2000; Lindblom & Woodhouse, 1993), examining the politics of policy making becomes imperative, particularly within the context of formerly colonised countries (Jordaan, 2001). The policy process would begin by looking at the operational material content of the legacy of colonialism, namely its structure and operations, prompting Cruikshanks and Huff (2000, p. 317) to express that:

> In many Other World countries [mostly former colonies]…
> in recent decades, most civil wars have involved assistance
> from outside states and served as proxies in global contest
> between the former Soviet Union and the United States.

Evans and Long (2000, pp. 64-5) presented the position that the primary function of the Other World countries (former colonies),

> as it was under formal colonialism, is to provide raw
> materials and cheap labour for the industrialized powers.
> [The] countries are now dominated by structures of
> neo-colonialism that differ little in substance from the
> colonialism of the past…[and] operate through the
> collusion of the Other World political elites, who have
> been co-opted into serving foreign interests.

Perceived or real external factors convinced the United States of America to consider invading and annexing Canada in 1812, and to attempt to overthrow Cuba's Fidel Castro in the second half of the twentieth century (David, no date; Hughes, 2000, p. 317). America's covert action in Nicaragua in the 1980s and open attack of Iraq in 2003 (Roskin & Berry, 1999, p.89) further demonstrate the role that the external factor plays in the policy process.

The central point is that economic and security compulsions dictate the policy direction and objectives of international relations. The inseparable synergy between security for one and security for all convinces states to join together in pursuit of mutual and collective protection against possible threats or challenges. In fact all regional and international groupings, namely the Southern Africa Development Community (SADC), Southern Africa Customs Union (SACU), Common Monetary Area of Southern Africa (COMESA), European Union (EU), Economic Community of West African States (ECOWAS), Organisation of Petroleum Exporting Countries (OPEC), not to mention the United Nations (UN), emerged out of individual and collective economic and security concerns. The member countries came together in order to secure trading partners, and to prevent conflicts among nations that were enjoying good political and economic friendship.

Yet, when two countries such as France, with a Gross National Product (GNP) of U$2178 billion, and Benin, with a GNP of U$4.44 billion (Countries of the World, 2005), seek collaboration, be it economic or political, it will be a situation pitting a very vulnerable Benin against insurmountable odds: the possibility of exploitation by a country (France) that could easily impose its will on the small nation were it not for the international deterrent in the form of the United Nations. Implied in such a relationship is that powerful external interests can easily influence policy formation in a small and largely poor country. Although some benefits accrue to the small nation, they will not in any way be comparable to what the big and powerful country gets out of the relationship.

Government policy process also experiences external intervention from within the country. Lindblom and Woodhouse (1993, pp. 25-31) presented that:

> With the interplay of ideas and suggestions from diverse participants representing a fuller range of relevant consideration…inequalities in power may give disproportionate weight to certain considerations, and some relevant views may go wholly unrepresented. [Consequently] action is undertaken not when a policy is proven correct, but when a working majority of those with influence over an issue reach agreement with each other.

The bases and sources of the influence are diverse, and their agendas different. If Africa is used as an example, it would vividly explain the fact that every country in the continent comprises regions, districts, and extended family communities residing in villages and/ or distinct areas, each with its own characteristics (beliefs and norms), as well as social and economic practices. Each clearly exhibits defined group interests. Lindblom and Woodhouse (1993, p. 75) defined such interests as 'interactions through which individuals and private groups not holding government authority seek to influence policy, together with those policies – influencing interactions of government officials that go well beyond the direct use of their authority'. Additionally, interest groups mobilise diverse viewpoints, factual information and other (policy related) ideas, and help to form a feasible agenda by clarifying and articulating what citizens want, thereby serving as a crucial source of information for policy (Lindblom & Woodhouse, 1993). One such influence on the policy process is the private (business) sector.

Conclusion

This chapter argued that policy process comprises national and regional politics, personal views, public sector interests, and the influence of external factors. The policy process happens within at least five different environments, namely natural, social, cultural, political, and economic. It is, thus, propelled by a diversity of interests and agendas, each with its own characteristics.

Additionally, every policy process provokes complex networking and hard-nosed positioning of the contesting views. The result is usually a compromise. The operational dynamics that characterise culture, tradition, politics, economics, time, and technology trigger the policy process. Figure 2 (page 11) indicates the policy process stages, and summarises what each stage entails. Nevertheless, the result is usually a compromise.

References

Balaam, D. V. & Veseth, M. (2001). *Introduction to International Political Economy*. (Second Edition) Englewood Cliffs, NJ: Prentice Hall.

Cloete, F., Wissink, H. & de Coning, C. (2006) (Eds). *Improving Public Policy from Theory to Practice*. (Second Edition) Pretoria: Van Schaik.

Countries of the World (2005). Retrieved 25 November 2008 from http://www.studentsoftheworld. info/infopays/rank/PNB2.html.

Cruikshanks, R. L. & Huff, Earl, D. (2000). Prospects for the Future. In J. N. Weatherby, *et al.*(2000). *The Other World. Issues and Politics of the Developing World*. (Fourth Edition.) Sydney: Longman.

Danziger, J. N. (2001). *Understanding the Political World. A Comparative Introduction to Political Science*. (Fifth Edition) New York: Addison Wesley Longman.

David, D. (no date).Why did Americans want to go to war against the British in the War of 1812? Retrieved on 26 October 2011 from http:ca.answers.yahoo.com/question/index? qid=20100414200315AAz8y55 Wikipedia

DeLue, S. M. (1997). *Political Thinking, Political Theory, and Civil Society*. Singapore: Allyn and Bacon.

Evans, E. B. & Long, D. (2000). Development. In J. N. Weatherby, *et al*. (2000). *The Other World. Issues and Politics of the Developing World*. (Fourth Edition) Sydney: Longman.

Fox, W., Schwella, E., & Wissink, H. (1991). *Public Management.* Cape Town: Juta.

Giddens, A. (1993). *Sociology.* (Second Edition) Oxford: Polity Press.

Granovetter, M. (1995). The Economic Sociology of Firms and Entrepreneurs. In A. Portes (Ed.) *The Economic Sociology of Immigration: Ethnicity, and Entrepreneurship.* New York: Russell Sage Foundation.

Greenberg, J. & Baron, R. A. (2000). *Behaviour in Organisations: Understanding and Managing the Human Side of Work.* Englewood Cliffs, NJ: Prentice Hall.

Henry, N. (2001). *Public Administration and Public Affairs.* (Eighth Edition) Englewood Cliffs, NJ: Prentice Hall.

Hughes, B. B. (2000). *Continuity and Change in World Politics – Competing Perspectives.* (Fourth Edition) Englewood Cliffs, NJ: Prentice Hall.

Jordaan, A. (2001), Quality of Life Index: Measure of Policy Success. *Journal of Public Administration* **36** (3). Southern Africa Association of Public Administration and Management.

Lindblom, C. E., & Woodhouse, E. J. (1993). *Public Policy Making.* (Third Edition) Englewood Cliffs, NJ: Prentice Hall.

Martin, N. (2007). Activist Slams HIV/AIDS Policy. *New Era. Newspaper for a New Namibia.* Windhoek, 27 July 2007.

Mawhood, P. (1993). *Local Government in the Third World. Experiences of Decentralisation in Tropical Africa.* (Second Edition). Pretoria: Africa Institute of South Africa.

Ministry of Regional and Local Government and Housing (MRLGH (1998). Decentralisation in Namibia: The Policy, Its Development and Implementation. Windhoek: MRLGH.

Munroe, M. (1997). *In Pursuit of Purpose.* Shippensburg, PA: Destiny Image Publishers.

Orwell, G. (1946). *Animal Farm.* New York: Harcourt Brace Jovanovich.

Parenti, M. (1978). *Power and the Powerless.* New York: St. Martin's Press.

Roskin, M. G., & Berry, N. O. (1999). *The New World of International Relations.* (Fourth Edition) Englewood Cliffs, NJ: Prentice Hall.

Roskin, M. G., Cord, R. L., Medeiros, J. A., Jones, W. S. (2000). *Political Science – An Introduction.* (Seventh Edition) Englewood Cliffs, NJ: Prentice Hall.

Schein, E. H. (1994). *Organisational Psychology.* (Third Edition) Englewood Cliffs, NJ: Prentice Hall.

Smith, A. (1994). *The Wealth of Nations.* New York: Modern Library.

Vansina, J. (1965). *Oral Traditions: A Study in Historical Methodology.* Chicago: Aldine Publishing.

Woodcock, M., & Narayan, D. (2000). Social Capital: Implications for Development Theory, Research and Policy. *The World Bank Observer* **15**(2).

Zanden, J. & Vander, W. (1990). *Sociology, the Core.* (Second Edition) Paris: McGraw-Hall.

4

CONSTITUENCIES

Individual, group and community expressions within given space and time help to explain the synergies among key elements that influence policy processes.

The structure of society is complex,' as Jordaan states (2001, p. 229), and embraces conflicting cultural, traditional and political values that 'serve as the motivation and driving force behind the quest of the state to maximise national security, welfare, prestige and power' (Olivier, 2006, p. 169). The complexity also serves as a habitat of important policy constituencies that symbiotically provide for individual 'desire to get ahead [as] a compelling passion in our world' (Munroe, 1992, p. 70). It happens within unending phenomena that symbolise social formations, group alliances, and a wide spectrum of social and political contradictions. Having stated earlier that policy making is a manifestation of politics in which egos vie for dominance, there is merit in arguing that politics symbolise power struggle (Roskin *et al.* 2000). Hence the quest to maximise welfare, combined with the desire to get ahead, manifest themselves through policies. That explains Roskin *et al.*'s argument that 'things happen not by accident; everything has a cause' (2000, p. 24). Culture, tradition and politics, as constituencies of policy, have clear causes and objectives. These are highlighted by the policy debates that seek to translate issues into practical action programmes with specific policy objectives and outcomes, prompting James Anderson (2003, p. 2) to define policy 'as a relatively stable, purposive course of action followed by an actor or set of actors in dealing with a problem or matter of concern'.

Culture

Manifestation of cultural influence in the policy process is multi-faceted, and is largely anchored in each individual's sense of belonging. That means 'what happens to individuals is a surface phenomenon' (Balaam, 2001, p. 74), because culture is characteristically deep rooted, and is structured by flexible practices concomitant with prevailing views on the size of the society (in terms of members) and territory, and its social, political and economic practices, not to mention norms and ethos. Since human practices are attestations of behaviour, culture becomes a major constituency of policy process, because policies are designed to control behaviour. Members' adherence to cultural practices is shown through various ways, which include kinesics behaviour (the body language of communi and paralanguage (the way things are said) (Ferreira, 2006); and the economics of affe – a natural compulsion to provide for those closest to you, and to alleviate econo hardships facing your kith and kin. These conditions play a pivotal role in influencin policy process.

Policy process could be referred to as a purposive call based on one's perception of life demands. Therefore, discriminating between possible viable policy alternatives is unavoidable, because not all contending issues can be served by one policy. It is an exercise that entails making choices based on moral preferences and judgment (DeLue, 1997), which are unavoidably influenced by the synergy between the individual and his/her cultural habitat, in terms of:

- identification with demographic properties, e.g. birth-place, language, and historical background;
- community peculiarities such as specific physical practices;
- norms, ethos and beliefs; and
- one's observed fate or punishment (comeuppance).

In the process, the factors that define and determine morality could be found wanting. Consequently, the need to survive determines an individual's perception of his/her habitat. In turn, the habitat provides life conditions determined by or prompting policies designed to enhance or sustain social and economic quality levels, focusing on the individual as the primary unit of life.

Hence, politicians see it as a natural duty to seek and satisfy their basic material needs as the first condition of life: even the holy ascetic must maintain his physical existence in order to continue his spiritual pursuit (Parenti, 1978). To that end, a public policy practitioner contributes as a stakeholder to his/her habitat and/or environment by first identifying with and responding to its dictates in an inextricable bond of loyalty to self, family, clan and tribal community, held together by demographic properties – a manifestation of a culture in a continuous quest for secure welfare, prestige and power (Olivier, 2006).

Tradition

As the second most important policy constituency, tradition is a special case of authority – the authority of the past (Newman, 2000, p. 3). It is yet another force behind the shaping and modelling of public policy. It commands compliance and rewards loyalty, in particular where there is a crisis of governance and millions of people live in abject poverty amidst economic affluence never before seen in history (Parenti, 1978, pp. 8-12). In alluding to the power and influence of tradition, John Stuart Mill proffered the view that:

> Human capacities are stunted to the extent that a person allows customs and traditions to dictate his or her way of life. Yet customs are not always necessarily wrong, but that, in living as they require us to, without questioning them, we desist from making choices about what is best for ourselves, and then we do not develop the kind of qualities that enable us to reach our higher capacities (DeLue, 1997, p. 200).

Tradition, thus, represents a collectivity of behavioural practices and output over time. Most importantly, it is an expression of consensus on the rightness of past practice within given territorial boundaries and group agreement that it should be continued, thereby adding to Johnson's (1966, p. 19) definition of society. He said

> [Society] is a 'moral community', a collectivity of people who share certain 'definitions of the situation' called values, which legitimize the inequalities of social organisation and cause people to accept them as morally justified.

By accepting and legitimising social inequalities, policy process seeks to find a workable balance without upsetting the prevailing equilibrium manifesting through the tradition's attributes. Yet he who venerates tradition cannot escape its compulsions to respect, oblige, and act in ways that uphold the tradition's perception of life. The challenge is that policy stakeholders are left with little space to explore possible alternatives. People must accept and practise whatever traditions they have. Therefore, policy can only explain human action by creating an environment into which human behaviour must fit, without depriving other policy stakeholders the opportunity to express themselves, and to define what is right or wrong culturally and contextually.

Policies inspired by the desire for good governance abound in every democratic country, but so do contentious issues with which epistemic communities grapple (Hughes, 2000). In the meantime, the debate on the nature of the public and private, regarding individuals' behaviour rages on, prompting endless disagreements on policy issues, even if there is broad agreement on the way forward. In that regard, DeLue (1997, p. 313) argued that:

> Individuals must be governed, no matter what their private values may be, by common public norms that are applicable to all citizens. In a civil society, accepting common norms means that all must respect the rights of all other citizens. Owing to this commitment, then,

persons must accept limits on how far they can press their
private values in the public realm.

Viewed within the context of good governance, the argument recognises the omnipresence of power struggle within social organisations or civil society, thereby underlining once more Hans Morgenthau's opinion that 'all politics is a struggle for power' (Roskin *et al.* 2000). Therefore, policy processes should be considered as political instruments designed to achieve acceptable standards of the well-being of the civil society. That means, first and foremost, that there should be a well-structured political system that exhibits the skills and comprehensive capacity to manage the affairs of the country. Kautilya once said well-being comes from living in a well-run kingdom (quoted by Roskin *et al.* 2000). That makes policy and politics inseparable. Each has a purpose that needs the purpose of the other in order to have a meaning in society.

Politics

Policy formulation is a manifestation of 'focussed' politics defined by Johns (1996, pp. 412-13) as 'natural expressions of life in organisations, arising from a rational response to a complex set of social needs and goals'. It could be argued, therefore, that political theory feeds the policy formulation process inasmuch as political theory is constructed with the object 'to put together a picture of the world that helps to explain the way it works' (DeLue, 1997, p. 1). Therefore, policy formulation has to unavoidably take into account domestic policy factors, essentially those characteristics of the people and their society, which include:

- political culture,
- the nature of domestic politics,
- forms of economic organisation,
- citizenry attitudes towards factors that constitute the overall environment; and
- environmental factors such as non-human characteristics of society, namely geography and geographic locations, topography/terrain and natural resources, and levels of technology (Beckman, 1984).

The synergies observed within the dichotomous and/or symbiotic workings of these factors – policy formulation processes, epistemic community formations, competing policy views, and political ideologies vying for supremacy in the policy debate – attest to the fact that politics as a pivotal policy constituency, sets the tone of the debate, the context of the issues, and the parameters of the policy objective and programme. Therefore, politics is not just a reflection of time measurement of past political and social conditions that have actually existed (Vansina, 1965), but is a constituency of policy, and a platform on which society, as erative factor in deciding upon the significance of events, attests to the consensus on values of the social system and its objectives for the future.

On the whole, society is a collectivity of vulnerability and strength, moods, desires, and demands. It is free to reject what is viewed as detrimental to the well-being of the citizenry, particularly in a democracy. It manifests through citizens as individual members of societal social collectivism, and as groups representing different social, political and economic formations and opinions. At the same time, the representation is anchored in the cultural, traditional (norms, values, practice), and political groupings of the stakeholders. Hence, there could be no better policy constituencies than culture, tradition and politics. However, time, corruption, and technology pose a serious challenge to the role of culture, tradition and politics, and their contribution towards human life longevity, in particular in terms of the extent to which each set influences policy process and the achievement of desired objectives.

Time

Time largely measures movement and activity defined in terms of the beginning and the end. It also provides a distinct space for every activity occurring between the beginning and the end of a policy process, if there is an end. Comprehensively, it refers to the relationship between natural and man-made happenings viewed as simultaneous, sequential, and intermittent in nature. The importance of time is that it gives meaning to each activity by relating it to a particular place and space within specific context and form. In addition, time indicates the appreciation and depreciation of value. For example, houses appreciate in value because the number of people in need of accommodation is always on the increase in a manifestation of the economic theory of supply and demand. The increase is an indicator that provides information on the value only after a specific time period. Similarly, it could be hypothetically argued that the value of university lecturers always appreciates because they gain experience by the year. The appreciation of their value results from their continuous reading of different academic literature and teaching in classrooms. By comparison, the value of movables – vehicles, office equipment and households – depreciates because they wear out as they are continuously used over time. So the longer the time, the less valuable the item becomes, because it loses its originality, except in the case of antiques.

In relation to culture, tradition and politics, time consolidates and entrenches the sense of belonging, commitment to the practice, and belief in the culture and ideology. Furthermore, time allows for the descendants of a stakeholder of culture, tradition and politics to submit to systematic social and political induction and impairment in that 'politics is a mechanism through which elites and others obstruct learning' (Lindblom & Woodhouse, 1993, p. 137), thereby insulating known practices and beliefs against possible challenge, modification or improvement. Therefore, the time factor in all policy processes is pivotal in defining the relations among the variables, and between the policy activities and their value to society. Time provides opportunities, scope, and duration for planned activities. It also affords evaluation of the activities, thereafter equipping policy makers with pivotal information to improve policy relevance. Time also allows for plotting the sequence of activities, thereby informing society about when and for how long each activity will occupy space. In turn, the activity and space relationship guides the process of analysing the cause(s) of the situation and how best to respond to the cause. The objective is to ensure that society is not disadvantaged.

The relationship between the policy cause and the process of determining what to do about it is anchored in the envisioned objective of the anticipated policy action. The response to the situation requires an understanding of phenomena, space, and the time relationship. One cannot think of policy formulation based on what, where, and for how long unless the what is clearly defined in terms of the relationship among its elements, indicating how long it (the what) occupied space. Comprehensively, time refers to the relationship between 'occurrence and activity' and 'the period in relation to other phenomena' within the context of movement or evolution. Most important to remember is that it begins with people because everything definable is explained only through human faculty – the mental capacity to identify the existence and relevance of objects/matter to human life.

Given the different identities that people have in society, and the division of labour between central government and local authorities, regional and institutional policies play clearly defined roles in every community. The roles apply to specific demographic areas, involving different behavioural identities, focussing on the 'whom', 'what', and 'where', thereby contextualising the policy issue. It backpacks demographic policy variables – identity, location, number of people involved or affected by the cause, the scope and extent of the activity or phenomena, including the culture and tradition of the people. Those involved must strongly identify with the policy during the period it occupies space, before claiming the practice as an endogenous evolutionary phenomenon differentiating one community from other communities. Most importantly, the practice must manifest within clearly demarcated areas. The concept of areas in this sense should be understood to mean geographical, professional, social and economic parameters. Each area needs space demarcated either according to geographical area or measurable period of continuous practice. The latter denotes duration or time – hours, days, weeks, months or years. Therefore, the ingredients of time are space, movement, duration, and human consciousness of these in relation to the phenomenon.

In the effort to understand the synergy between policy and time, it is necessary to understand that the existence of policy denotes place: demographic variables in terms of area, boundaries, and people; and policy implementation, translating policy articulation into different practical activities that should produce visible, tangible, and quantifiable results. Therefore, time, space, and duration constitute key constituencies of policy.

Quest for Development

Its quest to shape and control human behaviour entails that policy seeks to enhance life quality by comprehensively improving human security through consistent provision of goods and services in desirable quality and quantities, on an incremental basis. It also seeks to prevent unnecessary contradictions and conflicts likely to arise from competing egos, interests and different communities' social and economic objectives. Achievement of these objectives means the attainment of a higher level of development. Hence, the word development is nationally, internationally and, indeed, constantly on the lips of bureaucrats, academicians and students (not to mention politicians). The word is generally understood to mean sustainable incremental achievement of more and affordable goods and services that are qualitatively better than what is available today. That, for example, means putting in place modern drainage and sanitation systems, better medical and educational facilities, improved communication systems, and upgraded recreational and other social facilities, including houses. It also means an enhanced national capacity to create jobs and reduce unemployment; improved manufacturing skills; and the creation of an economic base for individuals and communities so they can be better able to purchase and pay for life requirements.

However, achieving the fit is usually undermined by the elites (social, political, and economic) who always 'have easier time preserving their advantage' (Lindblom & Woodhouse, 1993, p. 120). The major impediments are impairments that cultural and traditional indoctrination induce on citizens as they grow up. These are supported by corruption – an international cancer exemplified by the overnight collapse of the Enron Bank in 2002 (BBC News, 2002), not to mention the views expressed by Mobutu Sese Seko, former President of Zaire (now the Democratic Republic of Congo), who said that If you want to steal, steal a little, cleverly, in a nice way' (Mawhood, 1993, p. 32). These elites are sustained by greed at the expense of development.

In essence, the demand for development poses challenges to build national capacity; ensure local industrialisation; benefit from international trade; train one's own citizens on educational and economic issues; and ensure security, focusing on food, health, housing, political participation, and employment. Neither the conservation of culture nor the power of tradition has the capacity to withstand the challenge that these needs pose. This means that only good policies that enjoy broad political consensus can guarantee developmental success.

Technology

Whereas policy making is largely an exercise to gather and process information, technology has emerged as a very important tool that facilitates the quick collection and manipulation of data. Its exploits include digging and analysing archaeological material; improving available methods of research; the invention of new gadgets capable of better investigation, analysis and documentation; and undertaking research on humankind, our environment, and how to improve and sustain life. Technology also adds a very important dimension that reduces the time within which a cause of policy can be understood and an appropriate solution found. It is thus, a policy constituency in itself.

Conclusion

The chapter has focussed on culture, tradition, politics, time, development and technology as policy constituencies. Each of these constituencies has its own specific elements that characterise its contribution towards the success or failure of policy process. Their influence on the policy process has been given and their connectivity explained. The knowledge of policy process requires understanding the synergies of these constituencies.

References

Anderson, J. E. (2003). *Public Policy Making*. (Fifth Edition) Boston: Houghton Mifflin.

Balaam, D. N. & Veseth, M. (2001). *Introduction to International Political Economy*. (Second Edition) Englewood Cliffs, NJ: Prentice Hall.

Beckman, P. R. (1984). *World Politics in the Twentieth Century*. Englewood Cliffs, NJ: Prentice Hall.

Bovbjerg, R. E. (1985). What is Policy Analysis? *Journal of Policy Analysis and Management* 5(1).

Blunt, P., Jones, M. L. & Richards, D. (1993). *Managing Organisations in Africa: Readings, Cases, and Exercises*. New York: Walter de Gruyter.

British Broadcasting Corporation (BBC) (2002). Andersen Guilty in Enron Case. Retrieved 26 November 2008 from http://news.bbc.co.uk/2/hi/business

Danziger, J. N. (2001). *Understanding the Political World.A Comparative Introduction to Political Science*. (Fifth Edition) New York: Addison Wesley Longman.

DeLue, S. M. (1997). *Political Thinking, Political Theory and Civil Society*. Singapore:Allyn and Bacon.

Dror, J. (1968). *Public Policy-making Re-examined*. New York: American Elsevier.

Ferreira, G. M. (2006). Communication in the Labour Relationship. *Politeia. Journal for Political Science and Public Administration* 25(3). Pretoria: UNISA Press.

Hughes, B. B. (2000). *Continuity and Change in World Politics – Competing Perspectives*. (Fourth Edition) Englewood Cliffs, NJ: Prentice Hall.

Johns, G. (1996). *Organisational Behaviour – Understanding and Managing Life at Work*. (Fourth Edition). New York: Harper Collins.

Johnson, C. (1996). *Revolutionary Change*. Boston: Little, Brown and Company.

Jordaan, A. (2001). Quality of Life Index: Measure of Policy Success. *Journal of Public Administration* 36(3).

Lindblom, C. E. & Woodhouse, E. J. (1993). *Public Policy Making*. (Third Edition) Englewood Cliffs, NJ: Prentice Hall.

P. (1993). *Local Government in the Third World.* Pretoria: Africa Institute of South Africa.

₄. (1992). *In Pursuit of Purpose.* Shippensburg, PA: Destiny Image Publishers.

W. L. (2000). *Social Research Methods.Qualitative and Quantitative Approach.* (Fourth
ı) Singapore: Allyn and Bacon.

(2006). Ideology in South African Foreign Policy. *Politeia. Journal for Political Science and Administration* **25**(2). Pretoria: UNISA Press.

.ci, M. (1978). *Power and the Powerless.* New York: St. Martin's Press.

ɔskin, M. G., Cord, R. L., Medeiros, J. A. & Jones W., S. (2000). *Political Science, An Introduction.* (Seventh Edition) Englewood Cliffs, NJ: Prentice Hall.

Vansina, J. (1965). *Oral Traditions:* A Study in Historical Methodology. Chicago: Aldine Publishing Company.

5
POLICY PROCESS AND ORGANISATIONAL VIABILITY

As outputs of perceptions translated into goal-oriented programmes, policies are managed through consensual action, with an option to compel abidance if deviation is perceived to challenge acceptable life conditions in line with tradition, culture and common practice.

Policy process is the heartbeat of every organisation, not to mention government. It identifies the organisation with its vision and mission, and most importantly with its operational scope, strategies, and tactics, thereby indicating the overall format of the organisation's structure and programmes. It also implicitly indicates the quantity and quality of the human and material inputs, as well as the acceptability, reliability and trustworthiness of the organisation's output. Specific responsibilities are allocated to each and every office bearer as an integral unit of planned collaborative activities in an exposition of units' togetherness, mirrored through vertical and horizontal relationships as per task description (the execution of policy). Furthermore, policy process shows unity of purpose in a forced collusion of entities to serve the common interests of the organisation. Consequently, salient forces characterising different organisational structural levels manifest themselves. They include perception, coercion, political action, and personal integrity.

Perceptions

Policies emerge from information that reveals the nature of any given situation, particularly the relationships among policy process elements, such as demography, specific causes, and perceived danger and/or benefits to individuals, communities, society, country or organisation. These must be analysed and reconstructed in order to relate them to the factors of desired life. Normally, each policy stakeholder sees things differently. Not everybody would agree with the view that the ecological balance of nature is dependent on the imbalance of its elements – the differences and inequalities in size, movement, influence, gullibility, susceptibility, vulnerability, strength and all other attributes of identity and relationships. However, it could be argued that it is, in fact, these differences that provide not only the necessary balance, but the natural earthly organisation that guarantees the existence of each and every element.

Schein (1994, p. 15) defines organisation as 'a planned coordination of the activities of a number of people [or living things] for the achievement of some common good, explicit purpose or goal, through division of labour and function, and through a hierarchy of authority and responsibility', making the phenomenon a collectivity of elements in quest of a common objective. At the same time, each element needs space in which to exhibit its identity and life characteristics in an organised way as it contributes towards 'strong intra-community ties – bonding' (Woolcock & Narayan, 2000, p. 230). Wolves, lions, wild dogs and ants exhibit those ties. Their livelihood depends on how they organise themselves defensively and for the purposes of getting food, in a manifestation of bridging weak inter-community ties. The bridging of such ties also takes place with other living things (Woolcock & Narayan, 2000). For example, vultures thrive on kills by lions, tigers and leopards, and a wide range of small birds live on bothersome ticks that feed on the blood of large animals such as buffalos, in a triangular mutual relationship – weak inter-community ties or 'bridging' (Gittel & Vidal, 1998, in Woolcock & Narayan, 2000). As with animals, birds, and ticks, human society is unavoidably anchored in life-giving and reciprocally influencing (interdependent) variables, nurtured by particular kinds of relationship sustained over the time-equilibrium (Johnson, 1966), through organisation that is all-embracing socially, politically and economically, thereby establishing a social order in which different values and perceptions of reality exist in harmony. The objective is principally self-conservation dictated by a common interest to avoid violence (Johnson, 1966) and individual demise. The same is generally the objective of every organisation and government. It all results from policies.

Whereas the foregoing discussion alludes to self-propelling social formations, sustenance of the organisation points to the need to understand the nature of society, and that 'it is a form of order imposed by some men on others, and maintained by coercion' (Johnson, 1966, p. 16). The question is: are policies instruments of coercion?

Coercion

Coercion is generally understood to be the use of armed forces, paramilitary, police and other means to compel members of society to do what they would otherwise choose not to do. It is also considered to be an action resulting from planned policy purpose. Even the 'gurus' on policy formulation and implementation concur on the omnipresence of the element of coercion at every turn of the policy process. Starling (1979, p. 4) saw it as 'a kind of guide that delimits action'. In the view of Fox et al. (1991, p. 32), policy implies administrative rules and regulations that should be enforced without fail. Anderson (2003, p. 2) defined it as 'a relatively stable, purposive course of action followed by an actor or set of actors in dealing with a problem or matter of concern', while Dye (1978, pp. 4-5) saw it as 'a comprehensive framework of and/or interaction'. Easton (1953, p. 129) concluded that it is 'the authoritative allocation through the political process of values to groups or individuals in the society'. In looking at the key words of these definitions, namely 'delimits', 'rules and regulations', 'authoritative allocation', 'purposive course of action', and 'framework of interaction', one sees the pattern of legal compulsion for action to control human behaviour and organisational activities, through the use of policies as control instruments.

Clearly emerging from these definitions is the fact that policy is the heartbeat of every organisation and government in that it also helps to do the following:

1   Define the organisation's mission based on its objectives. It, thus, implicitly provides the programme of action by articulating the scope of activities.

    For example, if there was concern that people were being exploited by foreigners seeking permission to stay in a country through marriage to local citizens, a policy could be designed to control such marriages. However a system would need to be established to statistically keep track of the marital status of immigrants entering the country, in order to understand the factors, know the target group (age and social class), and how long such marriages lasted. Evidence from such an investigative exercise would inform the authorities so they could address the problem if such marriages were found to be exploitative in any way. The best remedy will be a closely monitored policy.

2   Inform internal stakeholders (government and Ministerial officials) about their individual and collective roles and responsibilities in implementing the programme designed to achieve specific objectives.

3   Suggest remedial action or measures to improve the quality of the internal stakeholders' policy output. That could be done through training, or through continuous research built into the monitoring and evaluation that accompanies the overall policy process.

4   Invite the policy consumers to embrace and participate in policy implementation.

5   Warn the deviants/dissenters about the consequences of non-cooperation or dissension.

These policy actions are expositions of organisational and administrative legitimacy provided by a national constitution to different arms of government at different levels. The levels include parliament and government ministries, or other statutory bodies such as provincial and/or district councils and administration offices (Mawhood, 1993).

In setting out the organisation's mission, the policy stakeholders, more often than not, 'do not share a dominant common purpose; instead, each [as a political participant] pursues some combination of private purposes and his or her own vision of the public interest' (Lindblom & Woodhouse, 1993, pp. 24-5). Personal agendas largely influenced by intra- and/or inter-community ties usually occupy the centre stage. They constitute a formidable force that, if not effectively countered by intervention from high offices, could derail the policy process. The phenomena usually highlight two important aspects of management, namely political connection and personal integrity, on the part of the personalities contending for dominance and victory in the ensuing policy debates.

Therefore, coercion is inseparable from policy process. It manifests situationally – directly, indirectly, overtly, or subtly. It can also be self-imposing through unwritten cultural and/ or traditional ways of doing things.

Political Action

As Lindblom and Woodhouse (1993) stated earlier, politicking characterises every policy issue, which makes good political networking a pivotal element of every policy process. This means that political action is a necessity for every policy process to succeed. Therefore, good relationships with individuals occupying high positions become a key and indeed a primary condition for both leadership and organisational success. 'Virtually all public organisations need favourable policy decisions and additional resources at critical junctures if they are to prosper,' stated Leonard (in Blunt *et al.* (1993, pp. 47-50). Using the Kenya Tea Development Authority (KTDA) as a case study, Leonard (1993, p. 48) observed that 'In Kenya and in most other African states, the relevant political intervention [that unfailingly makes policy process effectively operational] comes from the President.' The relationship between the KTDA's manager, Charles Karanja, and President Jomo Kenyatta in the success of KTDA's programmes demonstrated that point".

Personal Integrity

Finally, in almost every case, the mission of organisations is broadly to serve the community. Undeniable as it may be, the success or failure of that mission depends, among other things, on the integrity of the leading personality.

Loosely defined, personal integrity refers to the quality of character: a high level of honesty, an unflinching resistance to all unethical acts that discredit or bring disrepute to individuals or institutions, and an ability to convince co-workers or members of the community to have faith and trust in you. As Finkler (2001, p. 238) put it:

> Ethical behaviour bans conflicts of interest, inappropriate influence, bribes, working against the organisation, failure to disclose personal skill inadequacies, and failure to disclose important information.

Accordingly, Blunt *et al*. (1993, p. 49), in their study of political connections and organisational autonomy (also focusing on Kenya), concluded that

> the respect and support that a manager of a professional organisation received from his subordinates and from his peers in related organisations appears to be heavily contingent on his perceived integrity... Conversely, they felt free to slack in their duties if they were asked to do something by someone whose integrity they doubted.

Although not necessarily the all-embracing main requirement for effective leadership, personal integrity (if it is noticeable) boosts an official's leadership qualities in that his/her opinions will be considered and accepted as having been well thought out, thereby making it easy for that official to approach and present his/her case to high offices. Overt personal integrity also 'inspires the confidence of international actors' (Blunt *et al.* 1993, p. 50).

Given the above, it could be argued that organisation begins with a personal or group projection of life necessities that need to be consistently and reliably provided, in sufficient quantities to ensure the sustenance and conservation of communities. At the same time, the existence of communities is contingent on differentiated social, political and economic levels, based on parental lineage and demographic factors such as pollution, fusion (conjugation) and/or migration, and topographic demarcations (forced settlements proximity). Hence, an organisation primarily deals with numbers or quantities, locations, and delivery of necessities based on specific objectives. That said, it is necessary to look at the different levels of organisation.

Leadership and Operational Environment

As already mentioned, successful policy process is a product of political action. It requires good leadership qualities and managerial as well as personal integrity. Without integrity, one would find it difficult to convince colleagues on policy issues. In other words, policy process needs a leadership that inspires confidence and venerates truth and trust. Hence, underpinning policy implementation is the collection and processing of data on population, needs, location, and service delivery, using appropriate organisational instruments.

Important to remember is that organisational process does not happen in a vacuum. It is housed in an environment that provides a totality of life variables, namely land, minerals, rain and water, and ever-changing weather conditions. These are the primary sources of life. Of equal importance are culture and tradition. These are the primary determinants of behaviour in that they impart norms, values and common goals of a collectivity.

These environmental elements, and culture and tradition, are the foundation of policies. They provide the material requirements of life (land, minerals, rain and water, and vegetation), and the human requirements (culture, tradition and language). They also provide the reasons and justification for organisational activities necessary for determining needed goods and services through administrative instruments such as policies. Administration, thus, provides the platform for policy process in which theories and methods for sustaining, correcting, and improving life conditions provoke contentious issues and hot debates (Schein, 1994). It then remains for management to operationalise and implement the policy decisions emerging therefrom.

Since the purpose of organisations is to achieve specific objectives through human behaviour, and life demands largely determine human behaviour, policy becomes the bridge between the purpose of organisations, and the life demands of policy stakeholders, by trying to control human behaviour. It all happens within environmental factors that are attributes of nature (weather, topography, fauna and flora, and a myriad of underground minerals), working in conjunction with man-made situations (social, political and economic designs and structures). As organisational projectiles, the activities need operational framework and parameters in order to exhibit clear differences among policies. Hence, environment does not only influence the policy process, but it also impacts on organisation's structure and organisational effectiveness by providing verifiable indicators for its sustainability. In turn, organisational sustainability requires policies that respond to complex situations triggered either by nature or by human desires.

As already discussed above, the two factors that most influence an individual's designs on life are culture and tradition. They control people psychologically and behaviourally in ways that influence our involvement in the policy process. Furthermore, they are inseparable because together they project community identity, common practices, and beliefs. Hence, they influence individuals' perceptions about life. It is wisdom behind the policy, in terms of striking a balance between cultural compulsions and logical human actions, that makes an organisation viable or non-viable.

Perceptions entail interest in what is observably happening. They do not only affect individuals in one way or another, but also activate a chain of sensory reaction best explained by Weiten (1989) as being responsible for recoding, processing, storing and remembering information. Weiten (1989, pp. 106-45, 256-60), identifies the following:

1 the *'declarative* memory system', which handles factual information;

2 the *'nondeclarative* or procedural memory system', which houses memory for actions, skills, operations, and conditioned responses;

3 the *'episodic* memory system', responsible for chronological, or temporally dated, recollections of personal experiences;

4 the *'somatic* memory system', which contains general knowledge not tied to the time when the information was learned;

5 the *'prospective* memory system', which involves remembering to perform actions in the future; and

6 the *'retrospective* memory', responsible for remembering events from the past, or previously learned information.

As long as policy depends on recorded and processed information, it is important to know what to do about the situation as portrayed by the recorded information, and to remember to act on the information in the future. Yet knowing what to do, without considering the consequences of the action on the 'principle of equal liberty, may infringe on other people's rights. That, in fact, is the bottom line in as far as policy implementation is concerned, be it by a private organisation or by government.

Government is needed, and is indeed the biggest organisation in most developing countries. It is accountable to the civil society which, as Immanuel Kant puts it, 'is based upon the existence of laws, established and maintained by a constitution, to secure the rights of all citizens'. Kant stressed that:

> In a civil society, the principle of equal liberty is achieved with the proper use of coercion. This means that individuals have equal liberty to others only when there are juridical constraints in place; that is, legally binding laws that use coercion to ensure that people do not act as a 'hindrance to freedom' or as an obstacle to others having the rights they deserve. The laws must be designed to maintain a form of 'reciprocal coercion'…that each person is to be equally governed by rules and made subject to constraints, whose only purpose is to protect the freedom of all persons, equally (quoted in DeLue, 1997, p. 167).

Policies are made for that purpose: to provide equal protection and support to every member of the civil society so that they can receive goods and service equitably, thereby preventing individuals likely to be motivated in their day-to-day activities by non-moral push and pull factors impacting personal interests and desires (DeLue, 1997).

Organisationally, the connectivity of politics, economics, and the broader environment within which policy operates, is accepted the world over, even though there are differences in terms of ideology, organisational structure, operational scope, and levels of sustainability. Whatever the situation may be, it is communicated through political action in the form of policy to be followed or receipt of benefits therefrom.

Generally, political action is triggered by a lack of clarity regarding priorities, by different perceptions of institutional goals, uncertainty about policy output, conflicting group interests, and poorly defined courses of action (Greenberg & Baron, 2000). Political action aims to reliably and consistently provide goods and services in their successful mix and direction (Mullins, 1999). Not many people would argue that achievement of that goal does not indicate personal integrity of those in leadership positions. Unless the leaders are honest, trustworthy, respectful, ethical in their behaviour, and knowledgeable, society will question their integrity. In turn, the organisation's credibility will be undermined. Personal integrity is, thus, a very important force, along with coercion, political action, and perceptions that greatly influence organisational and governmental operations at every turn.

Perceptions, coercion, political action, and personal integrity are cornerstones of organisational viability. Perceptions entail views about the organisational complexity in terms of demands for appropriate planning and the planning exercise itself, the need to have clear and attainable objectives, the requirement for a well-organised infrastructure, the need for synchronised systems, the necessity to have sufficiently skilled personnel at all levels, and the need for adequate equipment as well as sufficient and reliable financial resources. Furthermore, perceptions facilitate research and the gathering of information that is critical for the overall operations of the organisation. Most importantly, perceptions provide for appropriate planning by identifying the indicators that can be used for data collection and use.

At the same time, organisational coercion through policies should be understood within the context of necessary action for achieving desired goals and objectives. Therefore, policies must have legal status and the binding institutional framework necessary to compel action and achieve what the organisation sets out to accomplish: to deliver goods and services largely through behavioural control. That could include the use of force, depending on the situation. By the same token, political action translates policy decisions into concrete programmes. It entails public political pronouncements designed to legitimise and create support for the policy programmes, in particular activities that aim to bring about the realisation of the overall policy objectives.

Finally, personal integrity provides policy process with high level acceptance of the policy's stated objectives and their envisioned value. People respect leaders who do not

Figure 4: In-built Policy Process Objectives

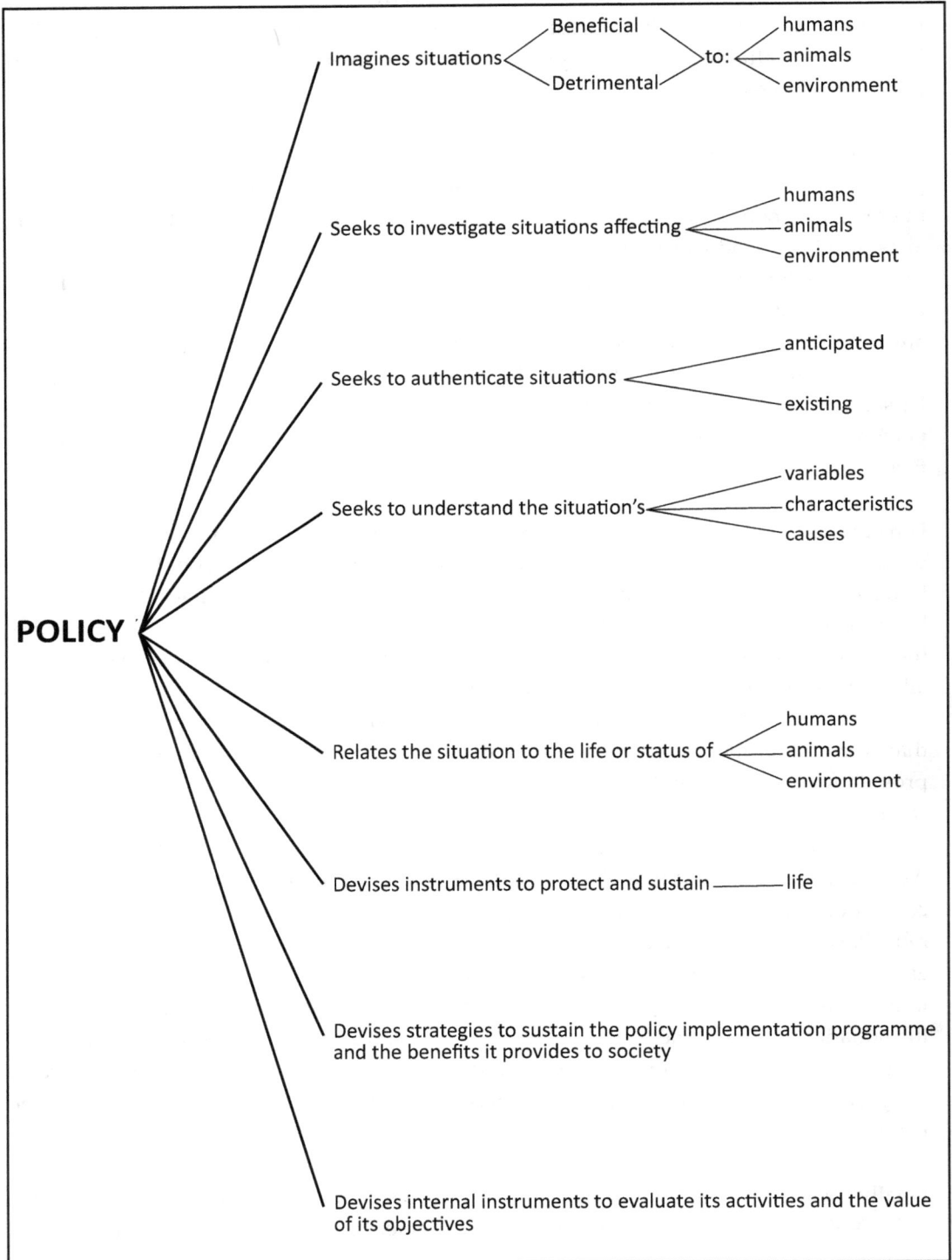

POLICY

Imagines situations — Beneficial / Detrimental — to: — humans / animals / environment

Seeks to investigate situations affecting — humans / animals / environment

Seeks to authenticate situations — anticipated / existing

Seeks to understand the situation's — variables / characteristics / causes

Relates the situation to the life or status of — humans / animals / environment

Devises instruments to protect and sustain — life

Devises strategies to sustain the policy implementation programme and the benefits it provides to society

Devises internal instruments to evaluate its activities and the value of its objectives have blemishes (or skeletons in the cupboard), and who have demonstrated sincerity, good faith and ethical behaviour in the past, and continue to do so. Therefore, policy process entails imagining or observing, investigating and authenticating situations, interpreting the findings, devising strategies and instruments for solutions, and evaluating the implementation and outcome as indicated under figure 4 on page 60.

Conclusion

This chapter argued that organisational viability greatly depends on the extent to which the leadership relates personal and group perceptions to the organisation's mission and vision. That accomplished, it is also necessary for the organisation to employ coercion, political action and effective networking if it wants to succeed in its endeavours. The latter requires personal integrity and recognition of the same by high authorities, as was demonstrated in the examples from Kenya.

References

Anderson, J. E. (2003). *Public Policy Making.* (Fifth Edition) Boston: Houghton Mifflin.

Blunt, P., Jones, M. L. & Richard, D. (1993). *Managing Organisation in Africa: Readings, Cases, and Exercises.* Berlin: Walter de Gruyter.

Cloete, F., Wissink, H. & de Coning, C. (2006) (Eds). *Improving Public Policy from Theory to Practice.* (Second Edition) Pretoria, South Africa: Van Schaik.

DeLue, S. M. (1997). *Political Thinking, Political Theory, and Civil Society.* Singapore: Allyn and Bacon.

Dye, T. (1978). *Understanding Public Policy.* New Jersey: Simon and Schuster.

Easton, D. (1953). *The Political System.* New York: Knopf.

Finkler, S. A. (2001). *Financial Management for Public Health and Not-for-Profit-Organisations.* Englewood Cliffs, NJ: Prentice Hall.

Fox, W., Schwella, E. & Wissink, H. (1991). *Public Management.* Cape Town: Juta.

Gittel, R. & Vidal, A. (1998). *Community Organising: Building Social Capital as a Development Strategy.* Newbury Park, California: Sage Publications.

Greenberg, J. & Baron, R. A. (2000). *Behaviour in Organisations: Understanding and Managing the Human Side of Work.* Englewood Cliffs, NJ: Prentice Hall.

Johnson, C. (1966). *Revolutionary Change.* Boston: Little, Brown and Company.

Leonard, D. K. (1993). The Secrets of African Managerial Success. In P. Blunt, P. *et al.* (1993). *Managing Organisations in Africa: Readings, Cases, and Exercises.* New York: Walter de Gruyter.

Lindblom, C. E. & Woodhouse, E. J. (1993). *The Policy Making Process.* (Third Edition) Englewood Cliffs, NJ: Prentice Hall.

Mawhood, P. (1993). *Local Government in the Third World.* Pretoria: Africa Institute of South Africa.

Mullins, L. J. (1999). *Management and Organisation Behaviour.* (Fifth Edition). Harlow,UK: Pearson Education.

Roskin, M. G., Cord, R. L., Medeiros, J. A., & Jones, W. S. (2000). *Political Science – An Introduction.* (Seventh Edition) Englewood Cliffs, NJ: Prentice Hall.

Schein, E. H. (1994). *Organisational Psychology.* (Third Edition) Englewood Cliffs, NJ: Prentice Hall.

Starling, G. (1979). *The Politics of Economics of Public Policy: an introductory analysis with cases.* Illinois: Dorsey.

Weiten, W. (1989). *Psychology – Themes and Variations.* (Second Edition) Belmont, California: Wadsworth.

Woolcock, M. & Narayan, D. (2000). Social Capital: Implications for Development Theory, Research and Policy. *The World Bank Research Observer* **15**(2).

6

POLICY PROCESS MAJOR CHALLENGES

> *Policy guards against behaviour that could be detrimental to consensual norms that underpin peaceful coexistence and development in society.*

If skills, technology and infrastructure are available, the major challenges to policy process would include a lack of information, limited financial resources, political intervention, personal agenda, culture and tradition, and implied commands.

Lack of Information

Information is central to every policy process because it informs the stakeholders about the character of the scenery and all other features of the problem or situation prompting the policy discussion. Hence, every policy process needs effective communication in order to comprehend and utilise the information received. Lack of information poses a challenge to the policy process in that policy consumers are denied the opportunity to fully understand the nature of the environment in which the causes of policy are found. This means that information lubricates the communication process, without which policy process is doomed. The policy environment is usually characterised by actors, activities, and time. These represent form and context, which in turn provide data as 'structured records of transactions…[with] no inherent meaning…[and] provides no judgement or interpretation, and no sustainable basis of action' (Davenport & Prusak, 2000, pp. 2-3).

Hence, data is key to every policy process because it represents concrete descriptions of activity or non-activity in the most neutral form. It does, however, need to be contextualised in order to influence policy decision making (Davenport & Prusak, 2000). The contextualisation is necessary for creating knowledge, or for creating 'expert insight that provides a framework for evaluating and incorporating new experiences and information' (Davenport & Prusak 2000, p. 5).

There are many reasons why policy process experiences a lack of the information or knowledge needed to tackle policy challenges.

Firstly, policy process begins with *initiation* – someone observing either a desirable phenomenon that needs to be protected for its value to society, or an undesirable situation that should be quickly corrected because it harms the general social fabric: all happening within a specific geographical area, or within clearly defined social, political or economic spheres of human activity. Those responsible for the needed corrective measures should always be mindful of the necessity for their actions' sustainability. However, the available information could be limited to symptoms, for example an influx of rural dwellers into cities is not the cause of rural unemployment; and a lack of interest in establishing various social services such as hospitals, schools, or different food outlets, is not necessarily caused by underdevelopment. The real causes could be that the absence of communication, water, and health infrastructure in the rural areas discourage companies with the potential to create employment from moving into these areas. Similarly, the quality of resources provided could be the main reason why people may choose not to go to hospitals or entertainment facilities. This means that people must be informed about the situation so that they can willingly take part in the policy process.

Secondly, accessibility of places with information does not guarantee availability of the right information in the right quantities. Informants can choose to withhold information unless they are paid, or they may have wrong information altogether, not to mention having the right information but very little of it.

Thirdly, the people – call them the right sources – may be willing to provide the information but may not be readily available at the time the information is needed. Yet, policy process can only be successful if the needed information is collected and processed within a specific timeframe. Therefore, a source of information that is willing to give the information but is not available when the information is needed is basically an unavailable source of information.

Fourthly, a combination of unclear purpose in collecting information, distance between the place where the information is needed and where it can be collected, environmental challenges, political interventions, and costs, can all lead to a lack of information.

These situations pose serious challenges to policy process in that they all deny the free flow of information and, in turn, undermine communication. Yet, the need, purpose and value of policy is expressed and understood through communication. Therefore, information is central to the success of policy process because knowledge about phenomena, and communicating the nature of the phenomena to the stakeholders, requires appropriate and sufficient information. Policy takes place only if the information required is available, is timely and is in sufficient quantities. The information should also be shared, which implies the need for an effective communication system.

Limited Financial Resources

Limited financial resources are as much a challenge to the policy process as a lack of information. The need for funds begins at the start of the policy process, with policy initiation. Offices, communication equipment, transport, data collection and processing, logistics, maintenance of infrastructure and salaries for permanent staff, all require money. These add to the complexity of policy process, which cannot be successful if it lacks adequate funding.

Although it may be easy to identify and isolate a problematic phenomenon or situation, it may not be easy to disseminate the information explaining the policy-related circumstances surrounding that assessment of the phenomenon/situation, unless one has the financial capacity to do so. Yet it is necessary to share the information with community members: those who were affected by the situation but do not know what to do about it; those who did not notice anything out of the common/ordinary day-to-day activities, but who would also benefit if there were a change for the better; and those who observed the unwanted situation and are eager to approach the authorities but lack the means (communication skills or transport) to do so. Communication entails the following:

1   gathering and organising information about the situation;
2   writing or typing the information;
3   determining the quantity of the information in terms of how much of it, where to distribute it, and by what means – leaflets, posters, letters, etc.
4   sending fax messages and to how many people?
5   making telephone calls and to how many people?
6   sending messengers and to how many places and by what means: car, motorcycle, bicycle, taxi, or on foot?
7   sending emails, but that requires a computer, which costs money;
8   travelling to different places to address meetings, but that requires transport, and people to advertise and organise the meetings, which also costs money.

Communication is a critical input for every policy process and all these methods require money. This means that you need money not just once, but for as long as the need to reach out for data continues to exist.

Since information dissemination is expensive, policy process requires reliable financial resources. Even government ministries cannot successfully complete their tasks without supplementary budgetary allocations and other contingency provisions. The demand for additional funding makes 'overhead expenditure' a permanent feature of institutional financial reporting. This means that all budget allocations are likely to become inadequate given the wide range of unexpected interventions, be they government, international monetary workings in their complex inequality of currencies, regional and national political settings (in turmoil or in peace), and the demands of natural phenomena – drought, floods, and diseases. Any one of these natural disasters can lead to a serious reduction or stoppage of financial support for one policy or another, due to unavoidable prioritisation and the transfer of resources to activities that are essential for human survival.

Political Interventions

Political dynamics constitute an important challenge to the policy process. They entail logical political action, caused by pressing social issues or matters that are important for human survival. They could entail taking an ethical action that may not be the right political thing to do at the time. For example, a medical doctor who is a member of a particular political party and at the same time a Permanent Secretary of the Ministry of Health could draw the wrath of parliamentarians from his/her own political party, or from the Parliamentary Accounts Committee, if he/she overspends the Ministry's budget allocation in the effort to save lives. At the same time, if the reason for overspending is indeed to save lives, it would clearly challenge the politicians' claim to be servants of the people. Nevertheless, the politicians will endeavour to steadfastly support earlier collective positions, particularly those taken in parliament, in the spirit of collective responsibility. In the first place, policies are collaboratively designed to provide goods and services equitably. Hence, it becomes necessary to equalise the capacity of the providers as they strive to achieve a workable balance in their duties. However, that could be torpedoed by unforeseen circumstances, leading to unavoidable actions believed, in the opinion of the operatives, to be ethically right even if they may be institutionally wrong. This is quite a dilemma! However, public problems must be solved. Public policy is a goal-oriented course of action adopted by governments to deal with such problems (Jones and Olson, 1996). At the same time 'individuals have been known to pursue political goals for other than egotistic gain, that is, for ethical ideological reasons, with no direct substantive benefit and sometimes with much risk to themselves' (Parenti, 1978, p. 8). Political dynamics, thus, pose a serious and continuous challenge to the policy process, and in many cases to the reputation of the policy formulators.

Personal Agenda

Personal agendas also constitute a serious challenge to the policy process, because they normally reflect the powers to which those involved in pushing them are egotistically attached. The view of those who push personal agendas is that life begins with them. John D. Rockefeller, Snr, quoted by Parenti (1978, p. 85) once said:

> I believe the power to make money is a gift of God…
> Having been endowed with the gift I possess, I believe
> it is my duty to make money and still make more money,
> and to use the money I make for the good of my fellow
> man according to the dictates of my conscience.

Personal agendas are not only motivated by money; they also emanate from cultural and traditional obligations. Historical practices, parental lineage, and community membership largely define an individual's position in society. That position obliges the individual to recognise, respect, and serve the interests of his/her own community members first. The allegiance spills over into responsibilities attached to stakeholdership of the policy process. The community membership, with its roots deeply sunk in the community members' collective history and the practice of the economics of affection, influences an individual's perception and comprehension of policy. Most importantly, it is how people want to be judged by the community that makes personal agendas a challenge to the policy process. It could also be argued that personal agendas emanate from an individual's perception of self. These factors do not necessarily have anything to do with whether or not that individual is a policy formulator or consumer. What is important is the role that he/she plays in the policy process, and what that role conveys to his/her peers and community members in general. The expectation is always that one should act in line with the community's cultural and traditional practices, which seek to achieve goals set by the common vision, and any deviation from the expected practices can land one in serious social and possibly economic problems, for example being ostracised.

Culture and Tradition

Culture and tradition stand out as major two-pronged challenges to policy process. Firstly, culture, particularly in Africa, entails a behavioural package that manifests itself through spontaneous group responses that reflect accumulated knowledge about the self and the collective community members, acquired through observation (Weiten, 1989). That knowledge could be defined as a social doctrine that represents a factual historical package, and gives meaning to the community members' identity. As a result, the doctrine influences the psychological makeup of every member of the community, and shapes his/ her response to external stimuli. Community members see and react to phenomena in ways that reflect their historical, cultural, and traditional acculturation, irrespective of their educational background.

Culture and tradition are attestations of group beliefs and desires, translated into observable actions deliberately designed to benefit all of the members who contribute to that particular culture and tradition. The beliefs and desires manifest through individual actions and community members' collective support of those actions. Examples include support when someone is in need of a job, financial or material help, protection against external threat, or counselling. Although expectations may not be written down, the mere belonging to a cultural or traditional group leaves no room for defiance. In fact, membership of the group makes it obligatory to abide by that group's behavioural prescriptions, prompting Greenberg and Baron (2000, p. 26) to state that African communities are generally 'collectivistic cultures whose members place a high value on shared responsibility and the collective good of all'.

It could be argued that the nature of the African cultural and traditional membership in a community makes collectivism a fertile ground for tribalism and nepotism, both of which are anathema to policy process. However, the compulsions for modern survival for any group of human beings are based on the establishment of a society generally defined as a population that shares the same territory and is bound together by economic and political ties (Brinkerhoff *et al.* 1997, pp. 92-3), in which the infrastructure of the economic production could be equated with that of Karl Marx's model of society (discussed in Macionis, 2001, pp. 96-8) as a pyramid of technology and social process of economic production as the foundation; on which social institutions (political, religious, education, family) are established; and the members of the institutions are bound together by ideas and values. These manifest within specific social, political and economic parameters as per the country's constitutional provisions and other legal control measures.

Furthermore, culture and tradition are an embedment of individual and group symbiosis, a veneration of very strong inter- and intra- social relations that thrive on political and economic osmosis, with a life that always lasts longer than that of an individual. Together, the symbiosis and osmosis directly impact on overall individual and group behaviour by shaping their perception of life, thereby influencing their output in the policy process. Hence, it is important to note that behaviour and practice are intrinsically intermeshed. They pose a conundrum like the question of whether the chicken or the egg comes first, in that behaviour is seen through action (practice), and practice is a manifestation of behaviour – a reaction to stimuli. Therefore, it follows that policy seeks to influence and/or control behaviour, and impacts on society – making people behave in a certain way in line with the policy objectives. Consequently, compliance entails policy relevance, acceptability and implementability. That said, policy acceptance and implementability are subject to ever-changing environmental conditions, and so are culture and tradition, although change may happen unnoticeably. Institutionally therefore,

> one thing is certain: the conservative continuities of
> authority and institutions that seem so immutable, so
> commanding, and so ubiquitous will themselves be subject

> to the forces of change. The human spirit, whether in its noble or aberrant forms, cannot be contained eternally in one particular set of social arrangements (Parenti, 1978, p. 229).

However, governmental policy change in terms of focus and target (redistributive policy typology) is a common phenomenon in African former colonies. There is no doubt that change will continue to be demanded when current policies outlive their purpose and become irrelevant.

Policy initiation or review requires courage, 'a capacity that enables people to maintain a steadfast commitment to uphold the basic values given to society by those who make the laws' (DeLue, 1997, p. 38), because culture and tradition host a mix of deep-rooted and broad-based conservatism. Although change is allowed to take place, it occurs at a very slow pace, and under close and careful supervision. It makes the institutionalisation of the redistributive policy typology a wholesome challenge to policy process, particularly given the propensity of advantaged citizens to resist change, because the quantity and value of what could or ought to be is abstract, and the value of current experiences is real and concrete. Socially, politically, educationally, and economically, redistributive policy typologies have been resisted in most African former colonies in ways that attest to the values of conservative cultures and traditions under discussion. As Casely Hayford stated (quoted in Angula & Bankie, 2000, p. 109):

> The African may turn socialist, may preach and cry for reform until the day of judgement; but the experience of mankind shows this, that reform never comes to a class or a people until those concerned have worked out their own solution.

Those who are concerned are the elites in charge of government operations. They represent a social doctrine anchored in the ravages of culture and tradition. They accept change only if it does not seriously challenge the norms and practices that the society set for itself. Yet, it is they who set the norms and practices that largely benefit themselves.

On the whole, it could be argued that cultural and traditional policy objectives are largely characterised by interests and threats. This emerges during heated debates on identifying issues to be put on the agenda. As Anderson (2003, p. 94) observed: 'The competition for agenda space occurs not only among those pushing favoured proposals but also between those favouring and opposing action on a problem.'

Agenda setting is the stage at which conservatism clashes head on with the forces of change (redistributive policy typology), usually in a spontaneous demonstration of deep-rooted cultural beliefs against strong proponents of policies that seek to improve the quality of life.

Implied Commands

Institutional or organisational politics largely involve social formations in a narrow sense – who befriends who, and what relations apply between or among what employees and why, leading to clandestine meetings and influences that sometimes affect hiring, promotion, and firing. Implied commands are, however, restricted to leadership preferences, mostly in terms of financially lucrative job assignments, including hiring. This takes many forms.

The majority of managers, chief executive officers, directors, and even permanent secretaries of government ministries know the rules under which they operate – the scope and parameters of their job descriptions. They are also aware of the consequences of unethical behaviour, particularly where it concerns organisational reputation. Therefore, they try not to do things that will publicly trap them in ways that compromise the organisation's public image. Furthermore, they would not want to lose their jobs. Yet, they cautiously and sometimes surreptitiously involve themselves in activities that can easily compromise the organisation, not to mention their own personal character and social standing. Employees are hired, promoted, or fired unprocedurally as a result of implied commands.

Personnel recruitment is professionally the responsibility of the Human Resources Management Department. The department will have rules and regulations that should be explicit, and provide modalities for executing the tasks of human resource planning as well as position determination and job classification, inclusive of remuneration, training and development (Andrews, 1988). These are tasks that newly employed personnel in human resources departments execute with commitment and zeal, but not without challenges. What can one do if the boss mentions his/her preference for a certain person to occupy a vacant post, yet that person does not have the relevant qualifications for the position? The boss may be very aware that the person does not qualify, and that there may be many other candidates who are highly qualified for the job. However, the boss might want the position to be occupied by his/her preferred candidate for social, political, or even economic reasons (the possibility of monetary kickbacks cannot be ruled out); and he/she might know it would be going against the rules and regulations of the organisation, and not want to be a victim of possible future enquiry should these unprocedural methods result in an investigation.

A boss can also use a relationship between a junior officer and a candidate for promotion to block the promotion, under the pretext that others would look at it as nepotism. Yet the boss might have his own candidate who also does not qualify for the position. It becomes very difficult for the junior officer to defy the order of the boss in such a situation.

When it comes to terminating someone's contract, every country has Labour Acts, which establish certain procedures that should be followed. However, a highly qualified person can become a target if he/she is seen as capable enough to influence peers and other employees to challenge undemocratic leadership. A boss can easily discuss the issue with junior officers in the human resources department, and create an environment that makes life unpleasant for the targeted individual. These things are done in ways that are suggestions, not open commands. For example, the boss might say: 'Since the organisation has once used so and so and she did a very good job, why not consider her for the position?'; or 'What if we try to balance the regional, tribal or gender representation by bringing in so and so?' or 'By the way that person attended the same University that you graduated from. If he joined us you could make a very effective team, what do you think?' These are effective strategies the boss might use to circumvent legal procedures without implicating him/herself. In fact, he/she would be protected because no explicit request would have been made, just a non-binding (but in actual fact binding) instruction in the form of a suggestion. Implied commands, therefore, pose a serious dilemma to policy process, and in particular to its procedural implementation, because they pit corruption against professionalism, and the politics of the belly against a guilty conscious – you had better respect the hand that feeds you.

Conclusion

This chapter discussed the major challenges of policy process. These include a lack of information, limited financial resources, political interventions, personal agendas, cultural and traditional influences, and implied commands. The chapter argued that it is necessary for these elements to work in tandem with the others in order for policy process to be successful. Any one of these has serious potential to undermine policy process, regardless of how well the process was planned.

References

Anderson, J. E. (2003). *Public Policy Making*. (Fifth Edition) Boston: Houghton Mifflin.

Andrews, Y. (1988). *The Personnel Function*. Pretoria: Kagiso Tertiary.

Angula, N. & Bankie, B. F. (2000) (Eds). *The African Origin of Civilisation and the Destiny of Africa*. Windhoek: Gamsberg Macmillan.

Brinkerhoff, D. B., White, L. K. & Riedmann, A. C. (1997). *Sociology*. (Fourth Edition) Paris: Wadsworth.

DeLue, S. M. (1997). *Political Thinking, Political Theory, and Civil Society*. Singapore: Allyn and Bacon.

Davenport, T. H. & Prusak, L. (2000). *Working Knowledge – How Organisations Manage What They Know*. Cambridge, Massachusetts: Harvard Business School Press.

Greenberg, J, & Baron, R. A. (2000). *Behaviour in Organisations – Understanding and Managing the Human Side of Work*. (Seventh Edition) Englewood Cliffs, NJ: Prentice Hall.

Jones, L. F. & Olson, E. C. (1996). *Political Science Research – A Handbook of Scope and Method.* New York: Addison Wesley Longman.

Macionis, J. J. (2001). *Sociology.* (Eighth Edition) Englewood Cliffs, NJ: Prentice Hall.

Parenti, M. (1978). *Power and the Powerless.* New York: St. Martin's Press.

Weiten, W. (1989). *Psychology – Themes and Variations.* (Second Edition) Belmont, California: Wadsworth.

7

THE WAY FORWARD

To succeed, public policy process needs to embody past experience, supportive civil society, effective communication, transparency, honesty and political will, and should enjoy a viable financial base.

Education on political honesty and transparency, involvement of civil society, borrowing from past experiences, and national economic development, plays a critical role in informing citizens why a particular policy is formulated. All the stakeholders must be fully informed, not only about the causes of the problem, but about alternative means of solving it, and about the objective of finding a solution through policy. Understanding the issues will make it possible to design the best methods of ensuring that the solution is sustainable. It is also essential to understand the importance of communicating what one learns about a problem and the value of the proposed solution to the problem, because a solution for one could be a problem for another. For example, decreeing a minimum wage far above what employers can afford to pay could exacerbate unemployment through retrenchment, and reduce absorption of school graduates by the labour market. Similarly, raising school fees in order to meet the cost of providing education could make it impossible for some parents to send their children to school. Hence, it is imperative to thoroughly investigate the cause of a situation requiring policy, before a policy is put in place. Therefore, policy process requires full information in order to ensure its success.

Although policy is formulated within the confines of government premises, it is achieved through cross-cutting activities outside official buildings. The causes need to be clearly identifiable so that they can be easily attached to factors of human life: initiatives, needs, threats, and natural phenomena that impact on life in general. Only then can a clear synergy be drawn between the purpose of policy as an instrument to control and direct human behaviour in response to the demands of human life: physiological needs, safety needs, affiliation needs, self–esteem needs, and self–actualisation needs (Schein, 1994), and the success of government and other institutions in terms of service delivery.

Policy Initiatives

Several centres of human activity provide futuristic policy initiatives that seek to improve the effectiveness of service delivery mechanisms, and the quality of the services themselves.

Policy initiatives are ideas prompted by the belief that the present life conditions can be improved. However, the belief must be based on concrete experiences such as deprivations – social, economic, or material of particular types – or a threat to life. The knowledge that the services and material can be provided if the government and the community organise themselves using available information to determine the necessary action, triggers policy initiation. The initiation itself entails gathering as much information as can be identified, and sharing it with those who are affected and who want government to address the existing but unacceptable situation. This means that the mere identification of a problem, the gathering and processing of information about it, and even the formulation of a policy, are not enough to address a problem. It is necessary that all the stakeholders be involved in the whole policy process. Therefore, policy initiation needs a broad base that facilitates inclusivity and sufficient consensus.

Political Honesty and Transparency

Politics is generally believed to be the art of identifying the best methods of providing goods and services to the population at large; ensuring equitable opportunity for individuals to freely participate in the process of national and local leadership selection and involvement in economic activities; and guaranteeing fair treatment before the law. Politics, thus, drive the activities of government, which is an institution comprising individuals bound together by a constitution that, among other things, stipulates their different roles in facilitating government's operations. Furthermore, politics is a manifestation of a people's history and vision for the future, a vision about how to ensure and sustain life fulfilment in economics, religion, education, and developmental activities in general. It cuts across the major environments that host human life, namely cultural, traditional, social, economic, technological, and natural. Each of these environments requires a specific political approach to address the challenges it poses to the effort to provide goods and services to the society. Inequalities in terms of available resources, and access to those resources, largely cause the challenges because the desire for access to the resources creates competition among those in need. At the same time, it compels government to play the role of a fair dispenser of goods and services, a task that is supposed to be carried out by a trained cadre of personnel committed to impartiality. However, the inequality referred to above may cause some of these cadres to serve their own interests first before attending to those of other citizens. Such temptations compel those who submit to them to act or behave in an unethical manner that challenges the values of society, in particular honesty and transparency. Their actions undermine government policies that seek to achieve fairness in dispensing the services that government should by right provide to all citizens. Roskin *et al.* (2000, p. 111) argued that:

> Each society imparts its set of norms and values to its
> people and the people in turn have distinct ideals about
> how the political system is supposed to work, about what
> the government may do to them and for them, and about

their claims and obligations. These beliefs, symbols, and
values about the political system [constitute] the political
culture of a nation – and it varies considerably from one
nation to another.

. same time, political culture presupposes consensual vision and belief in the
.isequences of doing things in a particular way. Its practice provides proof of a common
understanding and knowledge of the benefits it brings to the society. However, honesty
and transparency are behavioural qualities that not every citizen possesses. There are those
who are less virtuous, and who may seek to take material and monetary advantage of the
positions they occupy, through dishonesty and covert actions.

Involvement of Civil Society

Policy process comprises coordinated activities that are necessary to establish a distinct way
of behaviour in the society. For that to happen, the key societal elements, namely people
who eventually become implementers and consumers of policy, must be part and parcel of
the whole process from the beginning. Involving them from the start will reduce potential
criticism about the wisdom, purpose and value of the policy. After all, their views will have
been incorporated into the policy's motivational statements and overall programmes. The
citizens' involvement creates a sense of ownership that in turn bolsters acceptance of the
policy, and strengthens the citizens' willingness to partake in its implementation.

History world-wide has shown that preventing citizens from participating in any policy
process not only undermines development, but can trigger serious civil disorder and even
unseat a government. The events of the liberation struggle in Angola, the Democratic
Republic of Congo, Malawi, Mozambique, South Africa, Zambia, and Zimbabwe attest to
this view (see Nkrumah, 1970).

Borrowing from Past Experience

Although it might be felt that the world is a safer place today than it was a century or
so ago, Johnson (1966), White (1999), and Marsden (2008) argue to the contrary. Peace
remains relative, and is indeed an expensive commodity. It is largely denied by issues
of social, political, economic, and religious dogma, which are concrete constituencies of
human fallibility. Ireland, Eritrea, Ethiopia, Kenya, Korea, Côte d'Ivoire, Sudan, Togo, Iraq,
Jordan, Bosnia, the USA, France, Britain, all have or continue to experience violence of one
type or another – student protests, religious confrontation, military conflicts, and economic
discontentment (Europe Protests Rumble On, 2003). However, that is not to overlook
the successes of past policies. Globalisation is indeed today's buzz word because of the
collaboration of nations in many areas of development, guided by the shared and proven
policies of yesterday. Regardless of the environmental peculiarities, such policies are

applied with minimum adjustments. Therefore, it is important to note that if the p. that institutions experiment with today are successful, they will be reference point. future developmental endeavours.

Social and Economic Development

If the difference between what was and what is indicates an experience in which nature and human practices provide a joint quest and effort to improve life, then economic development is an attestation of human life elevated to a better and higher level. The prerequisites for development are availability of natural resources, material and equipment, well-qualified human resources, and good governance. However, the attainment of high levels of education is dependent on the availability of educational infrastructural facilities and teachers/lecturers, as well as national and individual capacity to pay for the learning process. Furthermore, the availability of teachers and lecturers depends on government policies that facilitate development of not only infrastructure, but the creation of a thirst for knowledge and skills for those who can afford it. In turn, the ability to pay for children's education is always a result of policies that create an enabling environment for job creation, thereby producing parents who want their children not to go through the deprivations they themselves might have experienced when they were young, but rather to enjoy a better life facilitated by the attainment of education that empowers one to find employment. Social and economic development is, thus, a chain of relations that explain that *what was* could not have been, had it not been for what preceded it; and *what is* could not be had it not been for *what was*. Therefore, what is going to be will result from *what is*.

Social and economic development mirrors synergies of the on-going practical life experiences that explain the value of policy process. It goes beyond the mere use of political influence and power –the capacity of leaders to 'use political resources so [that] their wants, desires and preferences successfully affect the actions, or predispositions to act, of others' (Jones & Olson, 1996, p. 50). In essence, that entails consensus: 'the extent to which there is [broad] agreement, at least among the majority, about basic political principles, institutions, and processes' (Weatherby *et al.* 2000, p. 80), which are necessary to influence formulation of policies that address issues of today in an effort to secure a better tomorrow.

Conclusion

The main argument of this chapter has been that policy process goes beyond the immediate object of controlling human behaviour. It articulates the synergy between politics and economics, or who gets what, when and how – politics and the production, distribution, and use of wealth (Weatherby *et al.* 2000). At the same time, none of these can be successfully achieved if the policy process lacks political honesty and operational transparency, if the civil society is not involved, and if past experience is ignored. These work in tandem.

References

Europe Protests Rumble On (2003). Retrieved 1 January 2009 fromhttp://news.bbc.co.uk/2/hi/europe/2873539.stm

Johnson, C. (1966). *Revolutionary Change.* Boston: Little, Brown and Company.

Jones, L. F. & Olson, E. C. (1996). *Political Science Research – A Handbook of Scope and Method.* New York: Addison Wesley Longman.

Marsden, C. (2008). New Protests in Athens, Solidarity Actions across Europe. Retrieved 18 January 2009 from http://www.wsws.org/articles/2008/gree-d13.shtml

Nkrumah, K. (1970). *Class Struggle in Africa.* New York: International Publishers.

Roskin, M. G., Cord, R. L., Medeiros, J. A. & Jones, W. S. (2000). *Political Science – An Introduction.* (Seventh Edition) Englewood Cliffs, NJ: Prentice Hall.

Schein, E. H. (1994). *Organisational Psychology.* (Third Edition) Englewood Cliffs, NJ: Prentice Hall.

Weatherby, J. N., Cruikshanks, R. L., Evans Jnr, E. B., Gooden, R., Huff, E. D., Kranzdorf, R. & Long, D. C. (2000). *The Other World. Issues and Politics of the Developing World.* (Fourth Edition) Sydney: Longman.

White, J. (1999). Worldwide Protests against US-NATO Bombing of Yugoslavia. Retrieved 19 January 2009 from http://www.wsws.org/articles/1999/demo-m30.shtml

8

CONCLUSION

Nature, people, and organisations, constitute a multi-faceted environment fertile for policy initiation in response to social, political, and economic behavioural compulsions.

Nature posits the first major policy habitat in that policy process involves diverse elements that include the following natural phenomena:

- *weather* in its multiple disposition;
- *minerals* in their diversity;
- *catastrophes* exposing the vulnerability of earthly existence;
- *topography* with its regional differences; and
- *diseases* as they continue to challenge humankind's scientific advances.

Every time each one of these phenomena attracts attention, or poses a problem, communities rise to the challenge, usually demanding institutional action in the quest for solutions. More often than not, communities demand that the government should put in place policies that control or direct people's behaviour so that they can avoid, prevent, or correct the consequences of undesirable situations. The policies are designed to serve for as long as the situation or problem exists, or is likely to reoccur. This actually means that communities need continuous education about policies, given the fact that change of residence entails new members coming into each area or community. In addition, the young need to be informed about the value of policies, because they are usually easy victims of problems that prompt policy process.

People constitute the second policy habitat, because they have the highest intellectual capacity to observe, understand, and analyse phenomena. They can take the necessary action to prevent adverse effects of undesirable situations once those situations have been detected. Hence, people's intellectual capacity serves our quest for survival through policy processes focussing on the daily needs and demands of life. In fact, these needs are the core causes of policy process. They come in different forms and categories, such as natural phenomena, physiological needs, and government's developmental priorities. These n different forms and at different times, best categorised by Maslow's hierarchy comprising the following:

> *physiological needs* – food, water, oxygen, and shelter;
> *safety needs* – security, stability, and freedom from anxiety;
> 3   *belongingness needs* – the need for social interaction, affection, love, companionship, and friendship;
> 4   *esteem and self-actualisation needs* – freedom to develop, to the fullest extent, one's competence and true potential as an individual, and to express one's skills, talents and emotions in a manner that is most personally fulfilling (Johns, 1996, p. 162).

The challenges of policies that seek to address these needs include prioritisation, availability of resources – particularly material, the quantity and quality of the needs, reliability and consistence of the resource delivery system, and the sustainability of the overall policy process.

Government institutions constitute the third habitat. These institutions are made up of people whose activities are largely obligations imposed by constitutions and other binding regulations contained in ministerial and council policy documents.

Figure 5 on page 80 portrays these policy habitats.

The synergies involving natural phenomena, human needs, and government or institutional relationships underline why each one of them is a major policy factor. Together these inform us that policy process manifests within a given space and environment, and seeks to address specific societal issues that relate to human survival – the provision of the needs discussed earlier, taking cognisance of incidental life requirements such as leisure and personal indulgence.

On the whole, policy process is about human survival. However, life has different determinants that operate at different levels. Specific elements of human interaction characterise the levels as indicated above.

Human life needs food, water, oxygen, and shelter *(physiological needs)*. Yet, in order to obtain these, an individual must have economic capacity. If not, then that individual must have support from somewhere. Both earning capacity and the availability of economic support are made possible by good economic policies that empower citizens, such that they either become employable, or can employ themselves by going into business. Being mindful of the requirements for establishing businesses, it would be accepted that isolated policy approaches are not sufficient to create a good business environment. Unless there are synergies involving education and training, affordable facilities, and financial institutions

Figure 5: Major Policy Habitats

NATURE **Natural phenomena elements** — minerals — catastrophes — topography — diseases	If *natural phenomena* happened in the absence of human awareness, then they would be inconsequential because no one would know about them. We have knowledge about catastrophes, topography, minerals, and diseases because we continuously formulate policies to try to provide for ourselves the hierarchy of needs necessary to sustain life. However, we cannot always control or overcome natural phenomena.
PEOPLE **Hierarchy of human needs** *1 Physiological elements:* Food, water, oxygen, shelter. *2 Safety elements:* Security, stability, freedom from anxiety. *3 Sense of belonging elements:* Social interaction, affection, love, friendship – maintenance of social bonds through group association; a sense of belonging to a community; and community practices such as culture, customs and tradition. *4 Self-actualisation:* Skills, talent, and satisfaction from using them – the need to fulfil one's life potential in an enabling environment.	*Human needs* constitute the foundation of survival that should be secured through the prevention of bodily harm; social, political, and economic deprivation; anxiety; and through ensuring one's membership of and acceptance by the society, in which an individual enjoys the freedom to show personal skills and talent that contribute towards community vibrancy and the maintenance of common values. The challenge is how best to determine, institute, and implement responsive policies that can guarantee the continued, reliable and consistent provision of needed goods and services, in the right quality and quantity.
GOVERNMENT INSTITUTIONS **Government institutions' mission** — to execute specific tasks — to sustainably deliver goods and services — to satisfying public expectations — to ensure national development	*Government* is unarguably the biggest institution in most countries. Its mandate is to respond timeously to societal challenges and needs, with the view to maintaining national unity and political vibrancy that guarantee economic development and the equitable distribution of goods and services. In executing this mandate, government also seeks to continuously generate trust among citizens because government's legitimacy lies in being accepted and supported by them as citizens and as voters. Hence, government's policies endeavour to comprehensively address the challenges facing human security.

Source: From Y. Andrews (1988). Maslow's Needs Hierarchy Theory. *The Personnel Function.* Pretoria: Kagiso Tertiary.

willing to provide assistance, self-employment is very difficult to achieve. As a result, citizens will lack security in terms of everything mentioned above, including education and health.

Absence of security undermines individual and community aspirations for a better future. Community members need not only assurance from policies that provide learning opportunities, but also support from institutions that play critical roles in people's lives, namely security outfits, financial organisations, and political parties, given their involvement in policy formulation at government level. Non-governmental organisations (NGOs) also play a critical role in providing security through the delivery of goods and services that government entities and other public institutions may not be able to give. Such provision of security helps to build a sense of belonging to the community and at the same time improves citizens' respect for a government that cares about human life.

The sense of *belonging* is built on one's acceptance by the group and by the community, thereby facilitating free interaction with other members of the community. The activity builds and nurtures affection, love, companionship, and friendship (Andrews, 1988). Consequently, an individual will feel free to develop and show his/her true potential in terms of applying learnt and gained developmental skills and talents. However, it requires organisation to effectively exhibit skills. That becomes the policy process object: *empowering and involving the citizens in the design and implementation of organisational policies.*

The quest to succeed, competition for survival, institutional desire to achieve set objectives, and government's obligation to provide national security, underpin the necessity for appropriate policies. The tasks conjure skills of various types but do not guarantee success. Even with the best of skills, policy process could still fail unless two sets of variables work in tandem. The first set comprises cultural, economic, natural, political, social, and traditional environments. The second set comprises perceptions, personal integrity, time, and technology.

Policy process is about observation, investigation, prediction, planning, programming, protection, maintenance, sustenance, prevention, and observation. However, the endeavour to initiate, implement, and evaluate policy comes with unending challenges that entail action all the way. This book analyses some of the major and intricate interactions and complex synergies involved in every policy process.

References

Andrews, Y. (1988). *The Personnel Function.* Pretoria, South Africa: Kagiso Tertiary.

Johns, G. (1996). *Organisational Behaviour – Understanding and Managing Life at Work.* (Fourth Edition) New York: Harper Collins.

BIBLIOGRAPHY

Ajayi, J. F. A. (1978) (Ed.). *A History of West Africa.* Volume Two. Aylesbury, UK: Hazell Watson & Viney.

Anderson, J. E. (2003). *Public Policy Making.* (Fifth Edition) Boston: Houghton Mifflin.

Andrews, Y. (1988). *The Personnel Function.* Pretoria: Kagiso Tertiary.

Angula, N. & Bankie, B. F. (2000) (Eds). *The African Origin of Civilisation and the Destiny of Africa.* Windhoek: Gamsberg Macmillan.

Astone, N. M., Nathanson, C., Schoen, C. A., Young, R. & Kim, J. K. (1999). Family Demography, Social Theory, and Investment in Social Capital. *Population and Development Review* 25(1).

Balaam, D. N. & Veseth, M. (2001). *Introduction to International Political Economy.* (Second Edition) Englewood Cliffs, NJ: Prentice Hall.

Bayat, J-F. (1993). *The State in Africa – The Politics of the Belly.* London: Longman.

Beckman, P. R. (1984). *World Politics in the Twentieth Century.* Englewood Cliffs, NJ: Prentice Hall.

Black, P., Hartzenberg, T. & Standish, B. (2000). *Economic Principles and Practice.* (Second Edition) Cape Town: Pearson Education.

Blunt, P. & Jones, M. L. (1992). *Managing Organisations in Africa.* New York: Walter de Gruyter.

Blunt, P., Jones, M. L., & Richards, D. (1993). *Managing Organisations in Africa: Readings, Cases, and Exercises.* New York: Walter de Gruyter.

Bovbjerg, R. E. (1985). What is Policy Analysis? *Journal of Policy Analysis and Management* 5(1).

Brinkerhoff, D. B., White, L. K. & Riedmann, A. C. (1997). *Sociology.* (Fourth Edition) Paris: Wadsworth.

British Broadcasting Corporation (2002). Andersen Guilty in Enron Case. Retrieved 26 November 2008 from http://news.bbc.co.uk/2/hi/business.

Case, K. E. & Fair, R. C. (1999). *Principles of Economics.* (Fifth Edition) Sydney: Prentice Hall of Australia.

Cloete, F., Wissink, H. & De Coning, C. (2006) (Eds). *Improving Public Policy from Theory to Practice.* (Second Edition). Pretoria: Van Schaik.

Countries of the World (2005). Retrieved 25 November 2008 from http://www.studentsoftheworld. info/infopays/rank/PNB2.html.

Cruikshanks, Randal, L., Huff, & Earl, D. (2000). Prospects for the Future. In J. N. Weatherby, *et al.* (2000). *The Other World. Issues and Politics of the Developing World.* (Fourth Edition) Sydney: Longman.

Danziger, J. N. (2001). *Understanding the Political World. A Comparative Introduction to Political Science.* (Fifth Edition) New York: Addison Wesley Longman.

David, D. (no date). Why did Americans want to go to war against the British in the War of 1812. Retrieved on 26 October 2011 from http:ca.answers.yahoo.com/question/index?qid=20100414200315AAz8y55 Wikipedia.

Davison, B. & Buab, F. K. (1966). *A History of West Africa to the Nineteenth Century.* New York: Doubleday.

, (1997). *Political Thinking, Political Theory, and Civil Society*. Singapore: Allyn and Bacon.

. H. & Prusak, L. (2000). *Working Knowledge – How Organisations Manage What They Know*. ge, Massachusetts: Harvard Business School Press.

). *Public Policy-making Re-examined*. New York: American Elsevier.

 v. (1981). *Public Policy Analysis: An Introduction*. Englewood Cliffs, NJ: Prentice Hall.

. (1978). *Understanding Public Policy*. New Jersey: Simon and Schuster.

aston, D. (1953). *The Political System*. New York: Knopf.

Europe Protests Rumble On (2003). Retrieved 1 January 2009 fromhttp://news.bbc.co.uk/2/hi/europe/2873539.stm

Evans, E. B. & Long, D. Development. In J. N. Weatherby, *et al.* (2000). *The Other World. Issues and Politics of the Developing World*. (Fourth Edition) Sydney: Longman.

Ferreira, G. M. (2006). Communication in the Labour Relationship. *Politeia. Journal for Political Science and Public Administration* 25(3). Pretoria: UNISA Press.

Finkler, S. A. (2001). *Financial Management for Public Health and Not-for-Profit-Organisations*. Englewood Cliffs, NJ: Prentice Hall.

Fox, W., Schwella, E. & Wissink, H. (1991). *Public Management*. Cape Town: Juta.

Garang, J. (1994). A Speech on the Challenges of Political Liberation in Africa, made at the 7th Pan African Conference. Kampala, Uganda. April 1994.

Gibbon, P., Bangura, Y. & Ofstad, A. (1992) (Eds). *Authoritarianism, Democracy, and Adjustment – The Politics of Economic Reform in Africa*. Uppsala: Scandinavian Institute of African Studies.

Giddens, A. (1993). *Sociology*. (Second Edition) Oxford:Polity Press.

Gittel, R. & Vidal, A. (1998). *Community Organising: Building Social Capital as a Development Strategy*. Newbury Park, California: Sage Publications.

Glaucon's contribution to the debate on Socrates' City, quoted in Reeve, C. D. C. (1992). *Plato's Republic*. Indianapolis: Hackett Publishing.

Granovetter, M. (1995).The Economic Sociology of Firms and Entrepreneurs. In A. Portes (Ed.) *The Economic Sociology of Immigration: Ethnicity, and Entrepreneurship*. New York: Russell Sage Foundation.

Greenberg, J. & Baron, R. A. (2000). *Behaviour in Organisations: Understanding and Managing the Human Side of Work*. Englewood Cliffs: NJ: Prentice Hall.

Guha, A. (1986). An Alternative Approach to Public Policy. *International Social Science Journal* XXXVIII(109).

Hanekom, S. X. (1987). *Public Policy: Framework and Instrument for Action*. Johannesburg: Macmillan.

Henry, N. (2001). *Public Administration and Public Affairs*. Englewood Cliffs, NJ: Prentice Hall.

Hughes, B. B. (2000). *Continuity and Change in World Politics – Competing Perspectives*. (Fourth Edition) Englewood Cliffs, NJ: Prentice-Hall.

Ingram, H. M. & Mann, J. E. (1980). *Why Policies Succeed or Fail*. Beverley Hills, California: Sage.

Johns, G. (1996). *Organisational Behaviour – Understanding and Managing Life at Work*. (Fourth Edition) New York: Harper Collins.

Johnson, C. (1966). *Revolutionary Change*. Boston: Little, Brown and Company.

Jones, L. F. & Olson, E. C. (1996). *Political Science Research – A Handbook of Scope and Method*. New Addison Wesley Longman.

Jordaan, A. (2001). Quality of Life Index: Measure of Policy Success. *Journal of Public Administration* **36**(3). Southern Africa Association of Public Administration and Management.

Leonard, D. K. (1993). The Secrets of African Managerial Success. In P. Blunt, *et al.* (1993). *Managing Organisations in Africa: Readings, Cases, and Exercises*. Berlin: Walter de Gruyter.

Lindblom, C. E. (1968). *The Policy Making Process*. Englewood Cliffs: NJ: Prentice Hall.

Lindblom, C. E. & Woodhouse, E. J. (1993). *The Policy Making Process*. (Third Edition) Englewood Cliffs, NJ: Prentice Hall.

Maathai, Wangari. (2009). Retrieved 19 January 2009, from http://wikipedia.org/wiki/wangari-maathai.

Macionis, J. J. (2001). *Sociology*. (Eighth Edition) Englewood Cliffs, NJ: Prentice Hall.

Mad Mike & Mark (2008). Animal Planet TV Channel.

Malawi Decentralisation Secretariat (no date). Malawi Decentralisation Policy. Lilongwe: Malawi Government.

Marsden, C. (2008). New Protests in Athens, Solidarity Actions across Europe. Retrieved 18 January 2009 http://www.wsws.org/articles/2008/gree-d13.shtml

Martin, N. (2007). Activist Slams HIV/AIDS Policy. *New Era.Newspaper for a New Namibia*. Windhoek, 27 July 2007.

Mawhood, P. (1993). *Local Government in the Third World. Experiences of Decentralisation in Tropical Africa*. (Second Edition) Pretoria: Africa Institute of South Africa.

Ministry of Education and Culture (MEC) (1993). The Language Policy for Schools 1992–1996 and Beyond. Windhoek: MEC.

Ministry of Regional and Local Government and Housing (MRLGH) (1998). Decentralisation in Namibia: The Policy. Its Development and Implementation. Windhoek: MRLGH.

Ministry of Youth, National Service, Sport and Culture (MYNSSC) (no date). National Youth Policy, Youth Growing with the Nation. Windhoek: MYNSSC.

Mondy, R. W., Noe, R. M. & Premeaux, S. R. (1999). *Human Resources Management*. (Seventh Edition) Englewood Cliffs, NJ: Prentice Hall.

Morgenthau, H. J. (1978). *Politics Among Nations: The Struggle for Power and Peace*. New York: Alfred A. Knopf.

Mukwena, R. & Chirawu, T. (2008) (Eds). *Decentralisation and Regional and Local Government in Namibia*. Windhoek: R. Mukwena & T. Chirawu.

Mullins, L. J. (1999). *Management and Organisation Behaviour*. (Fifth Edition) Harlow,UK: Pearson Education.

Munroe, M. (1992). *In Pursuit of Purpose*. Shippensburg, PA: Destiny Image Publishers.

Namibia: Epupa Dam Study, Kunene (1998). Retrieved 15 January 2009, from http:/www.africa.upenn.ed/Urgent_Action/apic.

National Food Security and Nutrition Council (NFSNC) (1995). Food and Nutrition Policy for Namibia. Windhoek: NFSNC.

National Planning Commission (NPC) (1997). National Population Policy for Sustainable Human Development. Windhoek: NPC.

National Planning Commission (NPC) (2004). Regional Planning and Development Policy. Windhoek: NPC.

National Society for Human Rights (NSHR) (no date). Assessing and Managing Environmental Impacts on Epupa Water Project in the Kunene Region of Namibia. Submission to the World Commission on Dams. Serial No. INS102.Windhoek.

Newman, W. L. (2000). *Social Research Methods. Qualitative and Quantitative Approach.* (Fourth Edition) Singapore: Allyn and Bacon.

Nkrumah, K. (1970). *Class Struggle in Africa.* New York: International Publishers.

Ojagbohunmi, G. A. (1990). Institutionalisation of Policy Analysis in Developing Countries with Special Reference to Nigeria. *Working Paper Series* No. 83. The Hague: Institute of Social Studies.

Olivier, G. (2006). Ideology in South African Foreign Policy. *Politeia. Journal for Political Science and Public Administration* **25**(2). Pretoria: UNISA Press.

Orwell, G. (1946). *Animal Farm.* New York: Harcourt Brace Jovanovich.

Otaala, B. (2003) (Ed.). *HIV/AIDS – Government Leaders in Namibia Responding to the HIV/AIDS Epidemic.* Windhoek: University of Namibia Press.

Parenti, M. (1978). *Power and the Powerless.* New York: St. Martin's Press.

Parker, C. (2003). *A Manual of Public Management.* Windhoek: Aim Publications.

Portes, A. (1998). Social Capital: its Origins and Applications in Contemporary Sociology. *Annual Review of Sociology* **24.**

Reeve, C. D. C. (1992). *Plato's Republic.* Indianapolis: Hackett Publishing.

Riots in Uganda (2007). Two Asians Dead, Temple Attacked. Retrieved 25 November 2008, from http://www.sepiamutiny.com/sepia/archives.

Robbins, S. P. & Decenzo, D. A. (2004). *Fundamentals of Management. Essential Concepts and Applications.* (Fourth Edition) Englewood Cliffs, NJ: Pearson Prentice Hall.

Roskin, M., G. & Berry, N. O. (1999). *The New World of International Relations.* (Fourth Edition) Englewood Cliffs, NJ: Prentice Hall.

Roskin, M. G., Cord, R. L., Medeiros, J. A. & Jones, W. S. (2000). *Political Science – An Introduction.* (Seventh Edition) Englewood Cliffs, NJ: Prentice Hall.

Rotberg, R. I. & Shore, M. F. (1988). *The Founder, Cecil Rhodes and the Pursuit of Power.* Johannesburg: Southern Book Publishers.

Saasa, O. S. (1985). Public Policy Making in Developing Countries.The Utility of Contemporary Decision Making Models. *Public Administration and Development* **5**(4).

Schein, E. H. (1994). *Organizational Psychology.* (Third Edition) Englewood Cliffs, NJ: Prentice Hall.

Smith, A. (1994). *The Wealth of Nations.* New York: Modern Library.

Southern African Regional Institute for Policy Studies (1995). *Masters in Policy Studies – Research, Dialogue, Policy.* Harare: Southern Africa Printing and Publishing House.

Starling, G. (1979). *The Politics of Economics of Public Policy: an introductory analysis with cases.* Illinois: Dorsey.

United Nations Organisation (1992). General Assembly Debates. New York: United Nations.

Uzoigwe, G. N. (1973) (Ed.). *Anatomy of an African Kingdom. A History of Bunyoro-Kitara.* New York: NOK Publishers.

Vansina, J. (1965). *Oral Traditions: A Study in Historical Methodology.* Chicago: Aldine Publishing.

Viotti, P. R. & Kauppi, M. V. (2001). *International Relations and World Politics, Security, Economy, Identity.* (Second Edition) Englewood Cliffs, NJ: Prentice Hall.

Walker, Peter, and Agencies (2008). Zimbabwe inflation soars to 2.2m%. Retrieved 30 2009 from http://www.guardian.co.uk/world/2008/jul/16/zimbabwe.

Weatherby, J. N., Cruikshanks, R. L., Evans Jnr, E. B., Gooden, R., Huff, E. D., Kranzdorf, R. & Long, D. C. (2000). *The Other World. Issues and Politics of the Developing World.* (Fourth Edition) Sydney: Longman.

Weiten, W. (1989) *Psychology – Themes and Variations.* (Second Edition) Belmont, California: Wadsworth.

White, J. (1999). Worldwide Protests against US-NATO Bombing of Yugoslavia. Retrieved 19 January 2009 from http://www.wsws.org/articles/1999/demo-m30.shtml

Wilson, M. & Thompson, L. (1969) (Eds). *The Oxford History of South Africa.* London: Oxford University Press.

Woolcock, M. (1998). Social Capital and Economic Development: Towards a Theoretical Synthesis and Policy Framework. *Theory and Society* **27**(2).

Woolcock, M. & Narayan, D. (2000). Social Capital: Implications for Development Theory, Research and Policy. *The World Bank Research Observer* **15**(2).

Zanden, J. & Vander, W. (1990). *Sociology, the Core.* (Second Edition) New York: McGraw-Hall.

INDEX

ABOUT THE AUTHOR

Tapera O. Chirawu holds a Ph.D degree from Howard University in the USA. He taught African politics and history at Maryland University, College Park in the State of Maryland; and provided lectures on the same subjects at George Washington University by invitation during Summer School.

Upon returning to Zimbabwe in 1985, he served government as a Senior Administrator responsible for policy processes and developmental land utilisation, and as a Senior Researcher at the Zimbabwe Institute for Developmental Studies (ZIDS) - currently a unit of the University of Zimbabwe - before moving to Namibia in 1992.

In Namibia he served as a consultant on cultural policies, and later joined the University of Namibia where he held the positions of Acting Director for the Centre for Public Service Training (2 years) during which he designed several training programmes focussing on skills development and policy processes; Deputy Dean of the Faculty of Economics and Management Science (3 years); and Department Head: Political and Administrative Studies (10 years). Additionally he did consultancy work for the Ministry of Regional and Local Government, Housing, and Rural Development; and for the continent-wide Africities Movement. He later spearheaded the establishment of the Namibian chapter of the Organisation for Social Science Research in Eastern and Southern Africa (OSSREA) and served as its country representative for five years. He also authored Namibia's National Voluntary Presentation Report focussing on Internationally Agreed Development Goals and Millennium Development Goals, presented at the United Nations in June 2010; and Namibia's 2011 White Paper on Electoral Review.

Dr Chirawu has authored seven book chapters and co-edited one. His work focuses on political formations, policy processes, land utilisation and strengthening democracy in Southern Africa. He has also written articles on Zimbabwean politics, and co-authored a book and two conference reports: one on developmental research and the other on urban growth and service provision. *Understanding Policy Domains, their Salient Forces, and Organisational Challenges* attests to Dr Chirawu's continuous contribution to the international body of political and developmental views and concepts. Currently he heads the Policy Matrix and Development consultancy based in Windhoek, Namibia.

www.ingramcontent.com/pod-product-compliance
Lightning Source LLC
Chambersburg PA
CBHW081741270326
41932CB00020B/3356